Read these stories
+ Become my

Next success story

Coach

# Our CORE Journey

## 52 Stories of Profitability Through Accountability

## The CORE Training, Inc.

Edited by Marvin King and Kelly Zientek

# Contents

# Foreword

We compiled these stories to inspire you in your own pursuit of greatness. In these pages, you will find the stories of REAL people who have struggled and fought and broken through the barriers of challenge. These are the stories of my coaches and my clients who have risen above frustration and defeat to achieve greatness in real estate and lending. And they did it with the support and the accountability that we provided them through elite coaching at The CORE.

I am honored to be a top mortgage representative and thrilled to be one of the top mortgage lender and real estate coaches. Over the last 14 years, we have helped real estate agents and mortgage lenders across the country work on their prospecting, build and strengthen their teams, and count their money as they increase their savings and pay off debt, achieving levels of financial freedom beyond their dreams. Our real estate agents enter The CORE at a minimum of $10 million in real estate sales. In 2014, our top client sold $85 million. We also help loan representatives with incomes starting at $250,000. In 2014, our top client netted $5,300,000.

If you want to see great results in your own business, if you want to improve your business and personal relationships, if you want to achieve real financial freedom... in other words, if you want to live a life of greatness, you must follow the path of greatness and do what great people are doing. If you want to see your name in this book someday, surrender to The CORE system.

**Rick Ruby**
**Huntersville, NC**
**April 2015**

# The journey begins...

# Rick Ruby

### Founder

### Principal Coach

**Location:** Huntersville, North Carolina

**Started The CORE:** June 2001

# Rick Ruby

Looking back on my journey over the past 35 years, I never had aspirations of making a lot of money. I just wanted to be good at something. I started in the furniture business at Art Van Furniture, delivering furniture in the back room. I thought it was the best job ever, making ten bucks an hour, using my muscles. We'd get the truck loaded in the morning, and we'd run through the route to get the work done early so we'd get to goof off.

We had this store manager, Dan Hendon. He was a really slick, sharp guy. He used to be the president of Van Dyke Clothing and a television evangelist for a while, so his delivery style was super cool, posh. I was really drawn to him. He told me I should be in sales. I just had no interest and didn't even think I could do it. He said that I had a lot of personality, that I was good looking, that he could put a suit on me and teach me how to sell. He told me that all behavior is learned.

One of the biggest lessons Dan taught me is you copy from people who are where you want to be. It was the first time I learned that, and it's funny because that is what The CORE is based on. I copied Dan because he was a really great salesman and a really sharp dresser. I would walk around and listen to all the other sales people pitch the couch, and I developed my own style.

Of course, copying and getting some theory is good, but then you have to have action. So I sold furniture for three years, working twelve-hour shifts, every Saturday and Sunday, almost every night late with two weekdays off. I did great, and got better every month, eventually getting into the President's Club. I loved the competition of sales. It reminded me of being on the field as a kid, out there competing. The thought of competing was almost as fun as the joy of winning.

In that time, I also got married and had my first two babies. We wanted to buy a house, and our Real estate agent referred us to a mortgage guy. This guy and I got to talking and he said, "Wow, you are a good salesman. You should be in the mortgage business."

I told him I was in the President's Club here. I made $28,000 last year.

He jokingly said, "Rick I'm the worst guy at my company, and I made $55,000 last year."

I wanted an interview, and he got me one the next day.

I went down and met with the manager – a typical bald, blue suit, red tie guy – and we talked about the mortgage business. I didn't think it was for me because he wasn't very dynamic and not what I was used to working with. So Pete introduced me to his top guy, Mike Tapman. Mike was funny, good looking, and dynamic. Two minutes after meeting him, he whipped out his paystub and showed me that he made $122,000 that year.

I got a job there the next day.

My journey in the mortgage business was like so many old schoolers. In the old school, they gave you a four-inch book that was the Fannie May guidelines, some business cards, and told you to go call on real estate agents. So we just called on Real estate agents, got deals, and of course because I didn't read the stupid book, none of my deals closed; they all got rejected. It was horrible. So then I sat down and read the whole book cover to cover and learned all the rules. The mortgage business is pretty simple: You have to learn about assets, income, credit, and property.

So I got in the mortgage business and I copied Mike. We spent so much time together. For me, you pursue greatness. You see someone who is good at something, and you hang out with them and copy them.

The problem was, Mike had that big year, and he kind of thought he was untouchable. So my career started taking off in my second and third year as his career was falling. He never seemed to get past that one good year. He carried that paystub around forever, like he'd won a gold medal, but it was kind of over after that.

I learned a valuable lesson from Mike: You never get to rest. You've got to go out there and pursue it and chase it all the time. He won the championship and it was over, but for me, there was always the next championship.

During my third year in the mortgage business I made $103,000. I remember looking at my W-2 and feeling impressed because Mike had made $122,000, and I wanted to catch him. I had some real estate agents that were really good friends of mine, and I just kept on that path.

Then I broke a builder. His name was Bill Scalabrino. We met at a poker game and became friends. I did everything with this builder – hung out, played poker, socialized, jet skied. He sold about 100 houses a year, so instantly my volume doubled from 75 loans to 150 loans just because of that one account.

I learned right there that you have to have the big account. The big accounts make life easy. Little accounts are hard to manage and hard to keep happy. You've just got to get the big people. That's when I started chasing whales. My career started taking off, and it just kept growing, and I did more loans and more loans.

I was working for a company called D M R, and I got

a call from the manager because he had received a couple of complaints about me. I was a very angry young man, very violent, swearing all the time, a lost soul. I went off on this manager, swore at him and told him, "Who do you think you are? I'm the top producer! The company is going to support me over you."

The next day the owner called me and fired me over the phone.

Soon after, I got the best call I ever had in my life. It came from Tom Hammond, who owns Flagstar Bank, and who is the greatest mortgage man of all time. He wanted to meet with me, so I went down and talked to him. Tom is about 6'7", big beard, big tough guy, a guy you can really be drawn to. He really was that father figure I'd always been looking for my whole life.

He said to me, "You know I'm really rich. I have 20 million dollars in the bank. I'm really, really rich."

I said, "Why are you telling me that?"

He told me, "I want you to want to get rich. You are driven. I want you to really chase the prize, and the prize is to accumulate wealth. The second thing I want you to know is that I don't need you. I am already successful; you aren't going to make me more successful. Your job is to enhance my company, so you cannot be the Prima Donna you've been. I already heard about what you did with that guy. I know him. I don't like him, but you don't ever treat me like that."

I decided right then and there that I was going to be a good soldier. So, I worked for Tom, and he taught me a lot about money, margins, and how to price a loan. I made a million dollars for the first time working for him. It was a great run and a great experience.

But the most valuable part of working for Tom was a lesson he gave me that I still rely on today. I tend sometimes to be so intense that I can disrespect people without intending to because I'm so focused on getting it done, getting the deal closed, getting the prize.

I had been with Tom a couple of years, and I had a pretty big branch. I probably had nine loan reps, and I was closing about 40 loans a month personally. I was making a lot of money off the branch and off my production. I was breaking records. My wife had stopped working, and I was living in a big house in Rochester – life was really good.

And one day, his secretary called my manager. Tom wanted to see me at 8:30 the next morning. I thought I must be getting a prize or an award. So I went into his office at 8:30, and I was sitting in the lobby when Tom came in. He walked right past me and into his office without saying a word.

I started thinking, "What the heck is that?"

His secretary came out and said, "He is so disgusted with you that he can't talk to you right now. You have to sit down right there until he calms down."

Then I started panicking. My idol was mad at me. You know what that is like when you disappoint your mentor – It's scary.

Tom finally brought me in and leaned forward on his desk and said, "Do you remember two years ago when I told you I was rich?"

I said, "Yes! That is what I like about you. I was inspired by it. I love it."

He said, "Well, I'm going to fire you."

I asked why.

He said, "You are disrespecting the underwriters. You're yelling at all the processors, and they are in here complaining. You know I don't like my girls complaining."

So I told him that they were just underwriters.

What he told me next has stuck with me my entire life.

He said: "That is where you are wrong. They are human beings, like everyone else. Just because you make more money than them doesn't mean you are better than them. You've got two choices: Pack your stuff and get out, or go down to the store and buy them all flowers, go stand in that bullpen, and apologize to all ten of them."

Remember, I was the number one guy in the company. I was the prince of the mortgage business, and he was asking me to go apologize to the underwriters.

So I sat there, and he said, "What are you thinking about? Either quit right now or go down to the store."

He didn't even give me time to think about it, which was probably a good thing. Sometimes when we think about decisions, we get ourselves in trouble. So I went to the store and bought flowers and apologized to all the underwriters saying, "I'm sorry I'm a knucklehead, I'm a horrible human being, and I apologize."

My head was hanging down, and Tom was standing there watching this go on, laughing while I was doing this. But later on he took me out for a beer, and it was a lot of fun. I learned a valuable lesson that it is okay to reprimand, but you have to hang out with them after and tell them you love them. That is where I learned a verse that I later found in the Bible that says, "Discipline without relationship equals rebellion."

I worked for Flagstar for a couple more years. Tom Hammond was my idol, and I would be running Flagstar Bank today if it wasn't for this: Three times I was the number one guy, and three times I found out he was paying people a bigger commission than he was paying me to do less volume.

Every time I would go to Tom and say, "How come so-and-so is making more commission than me?"

He would say, "Oh, I had to pay that to get him."

I'd say, "Then you should have given me a raise."

I felt he was out of integrity with me, so I left.

It ended up being a great thing because I went out on my own with two partners. We opened Golden Mortgage in the late 80's as a broker on the platform that the three of us would split the overhead and we would keep 100% of our own commission. We had no loan reps. It was just me doing a lot of loans, and a couple girls doing my paperwork, including Sharon, who had been with me 19 years. We were cranking out 60-70 loans a month. One partner left, and then it was just two of us. All of a sudden a bunch of loan reps started coming to me and saying they wanted to work for me. So I hired some loan reps and was making my own commission off my business and leveraged commissions off some of these other guys.

Around 1994, I got a flyer in the mail that said, "Never Chase Real estate agents Again." It was for a seminar with Joe Stumpf teaching the concept of working the database. At the time, I had never worked my database. I had been in the business 10 years, and I had 1,500-2,000 clients that I had never mailed. The concept of taking care of the people you already have and having them refer you was unbelievable. It just blew me away. At the end of the seminar, Joe Stumpf asked us to fill out some information about ourselves, how much business we did, who we were. Well, I was pretty cocky, so I walked mine up to him and handed it to him.

He looked and said, "Oh my God! You make a million bucks. I never met a loan rep that made a million bucks."

I told him I had done it two years in a row. I knew instantly that his program was right for me. I bought his best program and paid in full with a check for $6,000. I decided that I was going to surrender, and he would be my next teacher. Because I grew up with no education, mentors are really important to me, and it's really important that I am good mentor now.

I implemented right away. I start mailing two letters a month to my database, and all of a sudden my volume went up 50%. I started doing 70 to 80 loans a month, up from 40-50, and I was just swamped. I had a six- or seven-person team, 10 loan reps, and was making a million every single year.

All of a sudden Joe asked, "Hey, would you be willing to share on my stage?"

I'd never done that before, but I said, "Okay!"

So he put me in front of a 500-person audience with no training, no direction and said, "Get up there and do a good job."

I asked him to share with me two secrets.

He said: "Share pain, and be real."

I got up there and shared pain about my life, my marriage, my business. I was real. The audience went crazy, and I was hooked. That was in 1995, so that's 20 years I've been on stages. I probably see 5,000 people a year in audience participation groups. I love it, but I always share pain, and I am always real.

I worked for Joe Stumpf for five years, and he was really tough on me. I remember this one show down in Florida. We would have this victory cigar at the end of the show and talk about how it went. I remember I went down to meet him and he had a big stack of paper half an inch thick. He had someone transcribe four and a half hours of my speeches. There were all these little circles on the paper. He circled every time I said "I" or "me." It was an insane amount of times. I had gotten a standing ovation, and we'd signed up a ton of people, but he still ripped me up and down and said that I was the most selfish person ever met in life, that it was his program, not mine, and that I was trying to steal his thunder.

This was a great lesson because a lot of times as sales people we get so caught up in what we are accomplishing that we forget about the team doing all the work and all the people behind the scenes. And when you are selfish, you cannot be a good husband. I was just a horrible husband, and not a good father, working 80 hours a week, and just doing everything wrong.

Just before I left Joe, he brought in this guest speaker, a therapist named Richard Clark. Richard was this old guy who looked like Santa Clause. When Richard came in to meet me, he put his arm around my shoulder, and said, "We are going to get along great."

I said, "No, we ain't. Get your arm off me!"

Richard has gone on to be one of my good friends, but at the time I was just very mean to the guy. He did a breakout session on being authentic. He asked to write words that had to do with being authentic, and he taped them all over the wall. We came up with 50 definitions: honesty, integrity, character, doing the right thing…

He said, "Well, you are all wrong. I'm going to give you the definition of being authentic. The definition of being authentic is being true to your author."

As a teenager I had met Jesus, and then I had gotten away from it, but right there the light bulb went off: Jesus is my author, and I was not being true to my author. I was doing everything he says not to do.

In the middle of the room, in front of 100 people I broke down and started bawling. This was maybe the second time in my life that I have cried. The first was when I lost a son from a bad heart at a year and a half. I realized that I was not being true to my author, I was not being a faithful husband, I was not being a good father, I was not being a good leader. I was just being selfish, full of myself, arrogant, everything you don't want to be.

I went home that week and told my wife that we just could not be married anymore, that I was not being true to her, that I couldn't be a good husband to her, that I was going to take care of her financially because I had a lot of money, but that we were going to get a divorce. It just opened my eyes to a new way of living.

That was about 14 years ago, and it got me back on the path of chasing Jesus and doing the right thing. I decided right there that I didn't care if I never made money again. The funny part is that I make a ton more money now, but I make all my money helping other people.

Fast forward and now we've had The CORE running for almost 15 years. We have 333 coaching students that pay us $2,500 a month to coach. We have 31 coaches that are my true blue soldiers and warriors. I own part of Summit Funding with Todd Scrima, my partner at The CORE. I still run four mortgage offices: Brentwood, TN; Bloomfield Hills, MI; Cornelius, NC; and Fort Mill, SC. I have about 30 loan reps, and I close about 150 loans a month. Across Summit Funding, we have about 1,000 employees, and last year we closed $2.3 billion. I never thought we would be this big.

One of the most profound things Joe Stumps ever said to me was, "If you died today, who would be at your funeral, and what would they say about you?"

I told him maybe there would be 50 to 100 people at my funeral, and they would say that I made a lot of money, and that I was a really tough guy.

Joe asked me: "What would you like to happen?"

In my dream scenario I would have 400 people at my funeral, and they would say how I changed their lives.

Joe told me, "So start acting that way."

And that is what I am doing. That is what The CORE is really about: Helping people build structured relationships and structured teams so you can go off and be a husband, wife, and parent, and be in your community, and serve Christ, and find your purpose in life. The CORE is about living on a budget so you can save some money, buy some things that are fun, and make a difference on this planet. I'm honored to be a coach, that this many people would follow me and pay me to learn from me.

So that's my CORE journey. It's been an unbelievable journey, with 35 years as a sales person, 31 years as a mortgage man, 21 years as a trainer, and 15 years being a coach. I think I've been in all spectrums of the mortgage business, and there's no part of it that I don't know and understand. I think being in the mortgage business is a responsibility, not an opportunity, to do some really good things.

I've had 12 mentors in my life, and I want to leave you with four of them and the lessons they've taught me:

- ➤ **Dan Hendon**
  - o Dress for success
  - o Copy the people who are already there

- ➤ **Tom Hammond**
  - o Pursue greatness
  - o Charge a lot for greatness
  - o You can't survive without staff support

- ➤ **Joe Stumpf**
  - o Share pain and be real
  - o Live your legacy today

- ➤ **Roy Mason**
  - o Be a godly man in every aspect of your life

# The journey continues…

# Reeta Casey

## Principal

## Realtor Coach

### Location: Windermere, Florida

### Started with The CORE: January 2002

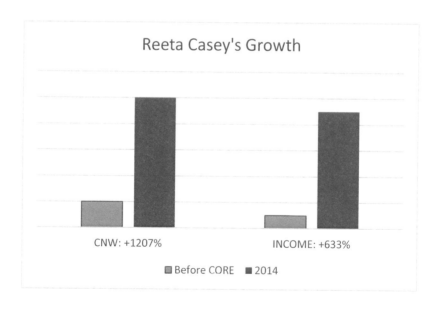

Reeta Casey's Growth

CNW: +1207%    INCOME: +633%

■ Before CORE  ■ 2014

# Reeta Casey

Wow, where do I begin? I met Rick Ruby 16 years ago at another coaching company. He was bold, loud, and direct. I loved his passion for helping people and he took me on to coach me on my business and my personal money.

I was a top selling real estate agent, but you would never know it if you saw my personal money. Every day was dedicated to my clients, listing houses, selling, and working 65 hours a week. Where did my life go, and where was the financial security I was supposed to have from my business?

Rick began mentoring me, and boy did my money and life change. I started working a structured schedule and learned how to build a team to cater to my clients. My hours dropped from 65 to 45.

Every month Rick looked at my CORE forms from tracking leads to personal money. This kept me focused on prospecting to increase my leads, closing for the sale to hit my closing for the month, and doing a monthly P&L to make sure my activities were on target to hit my goals.

I saw the biggest change in my money. In 2001 my family budget had a cash net worth of zero and no debt. Every single month Rick pounded me on selling and saving based on my dashboard numbers. It was painful, but when I see where I am now in August of 2014, it is absolutely amazing. Today we have $2.7 million dollars in cash with the option to "walk away."

For me paying the bills was the last thing I wanted to do; in fact, my husband, Pat and I would take turns at being responsible for this task, and we would each grow frustrated with doing it. Now, it is my favorite form because I watched our money grow and learned about the flow of money. How empowering and freeing to know we can grow our wealth.

Thank you Rick Ruby – my mentor, partner, and friend. I am grateful to God for introducing you into Pat's life and mine, and for the opportunity to be part of such a special community. The gift of financial freedom to take care of our families and of God's children is truly a blessing.

# Todd Scrima

## Principal
## Lender Coach

**Location:** Sacramento, California

**Started with The CORE:** January 2004

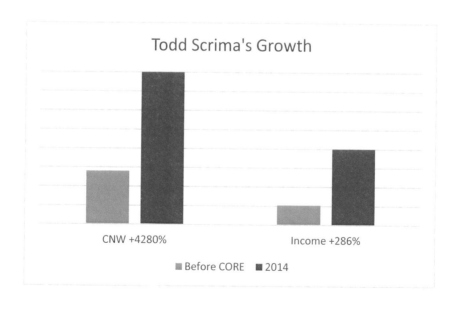

# Todd Scrima

My parents divorced when I was two years old; they both were remarried when I was four. We grew up in a small town outside of Redding, California, close to the Oregon border. My father eventually became a businessman. On my mom's side, where I spent most my time, we had a family farm. When I was 15, I started working as a janitor for my father's company. By 16, I was selling door to door, and when I was 17, I was selling and managing a few employees. I have learned about five major lessons that have helped shape my career.

**Lesson #1: Learn business skills early in your career. They will pay dividends for the rest of your life!**

My dad taught me a lot about selling, profit and loss, and people management before I was even 18. After graduating college, I went to work for my first mortgage mentor, a man named Jim Coffrini, who owns Sierra Pacific Mortgage. He taught me to call on Real estate agents, only do purchase business, and be out in the field five hours every day! He also made me read guidelines every day from 6 to 7 a.m. I was always pretty "coachable," and I just figured if I wanted to make a lot of money, I should do whatever he said because he made a lot of money!

**Lesson #2: Find someone who has the results you want and do whatever they say! Don't fight it, don't argue, don't complain... just do it!**

Of course I knew it all, and so I started my own little mortgage brokerage in March of 1995. I started with an assistant and a processor, and we were going to take over the world! By this time I was closing about twelve loans per month. I started growing my team, and over the next couple of years got it to an average of twenty loan closings per month. I was always aggressive in sales, I was genuine, and I truly cared about doing a great job.

I hit a wall in about 1998: I was working 70-plus hours per week, 30 pounds overweight, and starting to not enjoy my job like I used to. I had a Real estate agent who made me go to a Joe Stumpf event with him, and that is where I met Rick Ruby. After his talk, I knew I could learn from him, so I aggressively pursued him, and after getting on his schedule, sold him to let me come out and visit him for a couple of days.

We stayed up until 3:30 in the morning talking business the first night, and by the time I left, he had agreed to spend some time with me over the phone every two weeks to help me. We did not know it at the time, but this was the beginning of The CORE.

On the first call we had, I hung up on him and was pissed off. He told me I was a bad owner and needed to go to work for someone. I called him back the next day and apologized. He was right! This was one of my biggest lessons!

**Lesson #3: Ask for help every day of your life. Overcoming your ego is what is in the way of true happiness and results!**

Many things happened over the next several years. My mortgage company became a mortgage bank in 2000.

Rick, Reeta, and I began The CORE in 2001 and it was time to rock! When you start coaching the best mortgage lenders and branch managers in the country, you quickly learn exactly what works and what does not; this is a huge part to my success! I got married to Nicole in 2003, and we came home pregnant from our honeymoon in Italy. (It is a very romantic place after all!)

Every year I would do goal setting and vision planning with Rick. I was always creating pictures of what the companies would look like in five years, ten years, etc., running numbers, asking myself what skills I would have to develop to become a great leader and owner. I have learned how to manage people, I have multiple locations and deal with the agencies of Fannie, Freddie, Ginnie, as well as service loans, coach professionals, hedge loans in the secondary market, layer management, create long-term and short-term strategy, along with about 1,000 other things, which leads me to Lesson #4.

**Lesson #4:   You can do anything if you are willing to learn the skills!  If you are not, you will stay the same or go backwards.**

Today in 2014, I employ more than 1,000 people, have helped build the most successful mortgage coaching company with more than 300 personally coached students and thousands more in smaller coaching programs, and I run the best private mortgage banking company in the industry. I am able to keep my work hours under 45 a week, take four one-week vacations per year, and have a lovely marriage and family. I also squeeze in some golf and guitar playing!

My latest venture is taking everything Summit Funding does and all of our knowledge and building franchises similar to McDonald's (but way better). Today when we open a branch, we show them how to process loans, underwrite, recruit top talent, build a strong culture, and develop leadership skills and management skills so within two years it is closing 100 loans per month – totally unheard of in the mortgage industry!

Why do I work on all this when I don't have to? The answer to me is simple: I love helping people and creating something special! I believe retirement is a myth that most people want because they can't have it. I believe we are happiest when we are achieving and moving forward.

**Lesson #5: Have gratitude in your heart every day and love life!**

That's my story! At the end of the day you are who you hang around. I always wanted have a company with high relationship and high execution. At the end of the day, it's the people you choose to be around that make all the difference. I have been blessed to be around great people who love and care about one another, and that makes an exact 100% difference.

# Heath Barnes

## Lender Coach

**Location:** Houston, Texas

**Started with The CORE:** January 2010

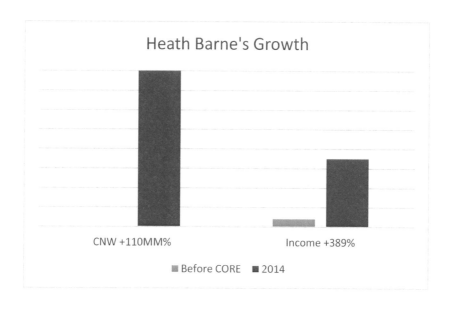

# Heath Barnes

A little over a year ago I was at home, positioned in front of my video camera, mentally reviewing a well-memorized script before I turned it on to rehearse, once again. I was presenting my pitch to become a coach for The CORE. And I remember thinking how it was still inconceivable to think how far I'd come since The CORE entered my life.

My transformation began when Jeff Wagner, my marketing rep, sauntered into my office about four years ago and asked if I had heard about Jennifer Hernandez. I asked what I needed to know about her, and he went onto say how she was being coached by a guy named Rick Ruby from a group called The "CORE." Jennifer and I had always had a friendly competition going on, and it was time I leveled the playing field. Within moments, I was on the phone with Travis Nichols, shelling out $2,000 with my maxed out credit card for a Summit in Austin, Texas. It was November of 2010.

Shortly after I signed up, I got a call from Rick Ruby and thought he resembled some kind of drill sergeant. He was brash and loud. After I told him how much money I was making, he said the best thing for me was to fire everyone – to get rid of my whole staff – and go back to being a loan officer.

I ignored Rick's counsel. But a little voice kept saying to me, "I wonder if what he's saying is true?"

Some background: At the time, I was paying my marketing rep 40% on every deal. He was responsible for 100% of all new business referrals. I was basically a refinance loan officer, and agents weren't sending me business. Well, maybe one or two were. And I was probably close to $200,000 in debt. My wife and I had just come off two incredibly difficult years, and she had no idea how deep in debt we were. I was unimaginably lost and wasn't looking at the numbers. I had no direction, no purpose, and no intent, other than needing to make more money. And I had no concept of what that even looked like or how to go about it.

The impetus behind going to that first Summit was again, Jennifer Hernandez. She always seemed to be doing well. She stood on stage and told her story, that after two years in The CORE, she had paid off $150,000 in credit card debt and had tripled her income.

Naturally, I wanted similar results, but I was still fearful of paying the $2,000 per month. And then I regrouped. I considered that it wouldn't make much of a dent in what I already owed, and if it was going to give me a lifeline to saving my business and probably my marriage, I was doing this.

At the Summit I was still bothered about the $2,000, but by the end of the weekend I was concerned with whether or not I was going to be chosen. In my interview with Rick, we discussed why I would be a good student and why he should choose me to coach. I sent in the previous year's tax returns, credit reports, all of it, and after a month, I received the call that I was accepted.

As I was walking my dogs, I was thinking that when the rates increased, there was no way for me to survive. I had no agents and wasn't tracking anything and didn't have a clue about how my business should be structured.

A month into my being coached by Brendan

Donaldson, my first coach, my marketing rep turned in his resignation. He had been with me for three years and it felt like I had just been punched in the stomach. A month after that, I was fired from the company I was working for, which meant that now 50% of my business was gone. It took me six months to really unwind, close down my branch at Republic State Mortgage, and move on. I moved to where I am today: Mission Mortgage. It was May of 2011.

So that I could change companies, I borrowed $50,000 from my wife against her 401K. I then recruited two people to go with me and do what Rick Ruby had suggested nine months prior. I was forced to take action. It seemed like there was a higher power directing where I should be, and it's a good thing I took the bait.

In the first year of being coached, I made more money than I had ever made in my life, going from $250,000 to $325,000. In my second year, I made $415,000 and in my third year, I made a little over $600,000. Last year, I made over $1,000,000.

All my debt was paid off within two years. My marriage has never been stronger. The team at Mission Mortgage began with the two I initially recruited and has grown to seven. We're looking at hiring around four people immediately and ten more over the next two years.

This is my fifth year with The CORE. I was coached for three and have been a coach for a year now. The CORE has given me resolve, purpose, and direction. It has transformed me into someone I hadn't known I could be. And in thinking about preparing that video presentation, I remember saying, "I will live up to your standards and represent you with the highest level of professionalism." I learned that from somewhere and have felt compelled to pass it on.

# Marjorie Adam

## Realtor Coach

**Location:** Charlottesville, Virginia

**Started with The CORE:** July 2006

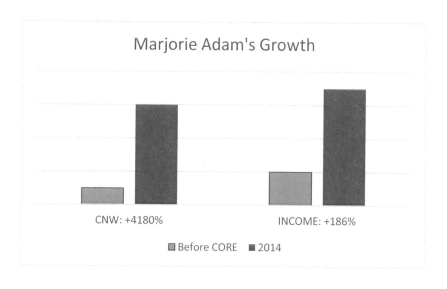

# Marjorie Adam

I got into real estate when I was 25 years old. I had gone to college and majored in photojournalism, so I had no plans to be a Real estate agent. After college, I traveled for almost two years throughout the country, living in a tent for five months and working many odd jobs. I spent one month in Alaska and slept on and climbed a glacier. I spent two weeks running the entire Colorado River from top to bottom, working as a cook's assistant. My family certainly thought I had lost my mind, but it was an incredible experience.

I then came back East and worked for about nine months for a small local newspaper. I covered the courts and police and general local news. I quickly realized that I would make more money working at the local McDonalds and would not smell like a newspaper, so this was not going to be a long-term career.

My mom was a Real estate agent, and I got my license and started to work as her assistant after I got married and moved to Charlottesville. I had grown up with signs in the car and visiting her at her office. My mom was a top producer and her clients loved her. She was known for her champagne lunches. She pioneered Break Breads before we ever thought to call them that. She celebrated with her clients and they loved her. While she was strong with Break Breads, she kept no database. Her clients, however, came back to her, because they knew she cared and she worked hard for them.

For the first couple of years I was a Real estate agent, I had three other part-time jobs. I worked as a florist, at a cooking store, and at a women's clothing store. It worked out pretty well. We always had fresh flowers at home, even in the bathroom. My husband is a chef, and we had just gotten married, so I got a discount to start up our kitchen supplies. I also had new clothes at a discount. I wasn't making enough to support just working in real estate. In fact, at the beginning of every month, we would borrow $600 from my mom. We would then pay her back at the middle of the month, and often borrowed it again the next month.

I slowly started quitting the part-time jobs as I began to make money in real estate. Pretty early in my career I started going to seminars. Early on, I learned the importance of having a database and keeping in touch with my past clients. I also started farming neighborhoods pretty early in my career. Back then, I would send more generic postcards with recipes or pretty front door shots, but I was sending them out, and most people weren't.

At this time, I had my first child, my daughter Alexandra in 1998, and also my son, Lucas, in 2001. I had them both in October, knowing it would not be ideal to have spring market babies. Yes, I was a planner. So my business was growing, but what I was not good at was taking control of my schedule. I was more of a Pop Tart Real estate agent. When the phone would ring and someone wanted to see a house, I was there. I worked pretty long hours and did not have control of my schedule. My business was growing, as was my income, but I was feeling pretty guilty about the time I was spending.

In the fall of 2008, I went to my first Summit. I had heard about The CORE for two years before going. I had gone to many seminars, so I was sure I would learn something, but did not realize that my journey was about to begin. It was pretty amazing to be able to spend so much time with Real estate agents who were amazing producers and strong business people.

I signed up for coaching after the Summit and after having a conversation with Rick Ruby. Rick called me and after asking me a few questions, told me that he could "fix" me. Frankly, at first, this really made me upset, as I was selling about $14 million a year and felt I was really doing pretty well. Most people, when talking to you about joining their program, tell you how great you are. Not Rick. He got right to the heart of what I needed to work on very quickly, and I respected that. What I had never focused on, and therefore had to fix head on, was my money. I was broken and in debt. It was humbling and embarrassing to admit this, as I really felt I had messed up.

As Real estate agents, we learn quickly that production is sexy. I, like many Real estate agents, had my "I Love Me" wall with awards and certificates. I won Salesperson of the Year in 2008. I was Top Producer many years in a row, and still am. However, no one gives you an award for being the best saver or having the tightest profit and loss statement. They don't spend any time in continuing education classes teaching you to run a profit and loss or a monthly business budget. You know that you need to pay quarterly taxes, but you are selling more every month and business keeps growing, so you feel it is okay to charge some more on the credit cards and save money next month. Before you know it, it is two years later and saving didn't happen.

When the market started to go down in 2006-2007, bills still had to be paid and less money was coming in, so I used the credit cards to pay many business and some personal expenses. I had some debt going into this time as well, and was not set with taxes. There is no greater stress, other than health or family issues, than debt. It is easier to just plug ahead and not focus on it than to face it and tackle it head on. Tackling it head on is what I did with the help of The CORE. From 2009 until 2013, I paid off over $120,000 in debt. I have not used a business credit card that I have not paid off at the end of the month since 2009. I learned my lesson. However, this lesson was painful. There were many mornings I cried in the shower and many conversations with my coaches about how to get through this. You get through it with a plan, and you get through it one month at a time.

One thing we all say we love about being Real estate agents or why we chose this career is that we love people, we love not having a set schedule, and we love not having a boss. The fact is, you will not succeed if you do not gain control of your schedule and learn to master time management. So for me in many ways, The CORE is my boss. The forms do not lie. You know you spent your time wisely or poorly after filling in your Greatness Tracker. We Real estate agents are all a bit afflicted with ADD. We see something shiny and we go after it. A new website? Sign me up! There is no better feeling than knowing exactly where your business comes from and being clear where to invest your time and your money.

The CORE has been a very good fit for me. I am a competitive person, and being on a call with other strong Real estate agents pushes me to grow. Winning the dragon for being the best student sounds like such a silly thing, but as my family knows, it's something I am very proud of. My "I Love Me" wall now features my dragons, pictures of my family, my son's homerun balls, and the paintings my daughter has made for me. My focus has shifted from my production to my savings, how much I spent, and my referrals.

The CORE is my real estate family. It is clear that if you surround yourself with the best, and you commit to doing the work, you will become better and better. There is no other program that I can think of that takes the best Real estate agents from across the country and allows us to learn from each other. We share everything, from our marketing ideas to our job contracts to our failures and our successes. You do not need to recreate the wheel. This is a proven formula for success. You just have to do the work. You have to surrender. Decide to be the best YOU that you can be, and work to make it happen.

# Brent Blaustein

## Lender

**Location**: Petaluma, California

**Started with The CORE**: July 2012

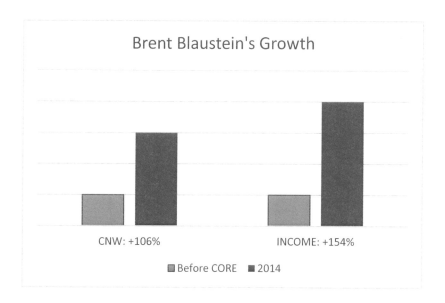

# Brent Blaustein

I was always a great loan officer. I closed on time, I under-promised and over-delivered, I had a strong following of Real estate agents and past clients that referred me business. Since I came from the operations side of the business, my confidence as an LO came from my ability to get the job done. My promise to never close late or ugly was my unique selling proposition.

However, I had no confidence in myself as a sales-person.

Three years ago, Rick visited my town for a Lunch & Learn for Real estate agents. I was lucky enough to be invited because the host was recruiting me. Other than the host, I was the only lender in the room. Rick was bold, brash, and not really my style at all, but as he started to talk about being a great sales person, I was hooked. I thought that if I could learn sales skills from Rick, combined with my technical abilities, I could explode my business.

And that is exactly what happened!

Unfortunately, I am a slow learner, and it took me a little while to pull the trigger. That day at the Lunch & Learn, I signed an interest form to attend the next CORE Summit in San Diego. This was only an interest form, and I wasn't immediately eager to part with $2,500 of my hard-earned money. Travis called me the next Monday and continued to call until I was ready to commit.

I attended the Summit and was blown away. I loved every minute of it and signed an intent form to start coaching, but at $2,000 per month, it was going to take a lot of convincing for my wife to sign off. We were getting ready to have our fourth daughter, and it was just not the right time to commit to $2,000 per month, even with the promise of increased business.

I signed up to attend the next Summit, and this time, my wife and I were both ready. She had talked to another CORE member's wife and was ready to support me. At the end of my interview with Rick, he made me commit to putting an ad on Craigslist that day in order to hire my first assistant within two weeks. Knowing what I know now, I can't believe I originated on the President's Club level for all those years with no help.

I am now in my fifth semester of CORE coaching and have just graduated from the two-year program. I have three loan partners, a junior loan officer, and two senior loan officers working in my branch. My income has almost tripled. Last year I reported $710,000 on my W-2's. My total net worth is over $1 million.

This program is truly amazing. It has changed my business and personal life in so many ways. I have learned to be a better leader to my team as well as husband and father to my family. I have learned how to manage my money and accumulate wealth. I have learned how to run my business like a business. I feel like I am a part of something larger than myself.

I love my life!

# Aaron Denton

## Lender

## Location: Cincinnati, Ohio

## Started with The CORE: January 2015

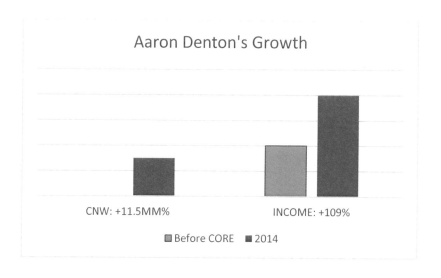

# Aaron Denton

I got in the mortgage business back in 2001. I had no industry experience, and I knew nothing at all about mortgages, but I had been doing sales a long time. I started when I was eight years old with a paper route. Over the six or eight years that I had that route, I sold something probably to all 110 people on my route, whether it was my door-to-door yard sales that I would do out of my wagon or a fundraiser for school.

So when I got into the mortgage business in 2001, I immediately put my sales skills to use, and within the first six months, I became the number one loan officer for that company. Being also the youngest loan officer there, that made me lots of friends...trust me. After a couple of years, I moved on to a larger brokerage, and again, became the number one loan officer.

In 2008, I was having what I thought was a lot of success to the point where I went out on my own and opened my first net branch, quit with my personal production, and went into full-time management. I was making around $250,000-$300,000 a year, which I thought was a pretty exceptional income. I'd only heard of one guy ever making $1 million in this industry, and that was back in the early 2000s at the height of the refinance boom. So, I always thought that it was an anomaly and that guy had just had a lucky run.

I grew up in the business with a transactional-based, marketing-based model. Everything that I'd ever been taught about how to get business was centered on marketing of some sort, whether it be direct mail, Internet marketing, tele-marketing, calling lists, or mailing lists. It was all transactional based, nothing relationship-based, nothing referral-based.

When I opened my first office, I did it on a bit of a budget, having never opened my own business before, and I got all my furniture on Craigslist. A few of my loan officers and I took a U-haul truck over only to realize that it was another mortgage only to realize it was another mortgage company downsizing and moving.

We got to talking to the owner. My loan officers asked him, "What kind of leads do you guys do here?"

I remember him saying that "leads were a bad word in his business." He didn't do leads. Instead, they got their business from Real estate agent referrals. We drove back to the office and we were literally laughing at this guy and how foolish he seemed. I remember I made the exact comment I made:

"Why would we want to go chase Real estate agents when we can drop mail sitting in the comfort of our office all day and close as many loans as we want to?"

Looking back now, I could just strangle the guy who made that comment. He was so arrogant, so full of himself, and thought that he had everything figured out, when in all reality, he had really no clue whatsoever. I had taken the only business model I knew and thought that I had perfected it. We did do a lot of loans. The part that is never mentioned is that in 2012 I spent $1.2 million on marketing alone. While I did have a profitable year, it was very, very stressful.

What I started to realize at the end of 2012 was that it was not a sustainable business model. It was a model strictly dependent on refinances and the market. If rates stayed low, it was a good business model. If rates went up, it was a terrible business model that resulted in catastrophic, explosive, no good events that could crash your business.

I'm a self-taught guy. I have an eighth-grade education. I dropped out of high school freshman year. Everything I know about this business, I taught myself, but I had never known how to do business in a relationship-based, referral-based model. I'd never really seen how to do this model. So I started seeking out coaching programs.

The first program I found was a company by the name of Xinnix. I flew myself and a few of my loan officers to their three-day workshop. We definitely learned some concepts that we were not familiar with and saw some things that we had never seen put in place before. The problem that I had with it was that all the guys who taught it and all the coaches in the program -- that's what they did for a living.

I thought, "Why are you sitting here making $60,000 a year telling us how to do it? Why aren't you out there doing it on your own?"

And of course they had their glory stories of all the money they'd made in '04 and '05 and '06, but in my opinion, this wasn't even the same business as it was at that time. It was an entirely different animal, and it was getting ready to make an entirely different turn from the last five years. I knew rates were going to go up, I knew purchase business was where it was at, but I had no clue as to the best, most effective way to go out and get it.

So I continued looking, and by luck, was referred to a company called The CORE. I flew out to a Mega event where they had six or eight coaches stand up and tell their story of how they got into the business. They told what their production was prior to The CORE and since their introduction to it.

The person who really stuck with me was Shayla Gifford. Shayla and I have semi-similar stories. We are around the same age, got into the business around the same time, and had come from producing a large volume of loans, working a large amount of hours, and making what we thought was pretty good income. So when I heard her story that the year before she got in The CORE she was working 80 hours a week and was really a slave to her business, and had gone from making $240,000 to $2.2 million in just two short years, I was definitely intrigued.

We came to the end of the event and they introduced their best student that year, a man by the name of Scott Forman. Now I had heard of a guy by that name in years past when I opened my first net branch because he ran a branch out of Jersey, so I'd seen this guy's production numbers before. At the time, they were similar to mine. I had competed indirectly with him; some months he was better than me, some months I was better than him. I'd never really met him first hand, but he was reality for me. He was someone I knew from my life. I knew his story, his old model and his production numbers, so when I saw him speak at the Mega and heard that he had gone from making $300,000 a year to more than $3.2 million on his W-2s, I was in.

I was excited, I was giddy, and I was ready to get into coaching. I went to sign up and found out:

Oh, you can't sign up here.

You have to give us a W-2 showing $250,000.

This intrigued me even more. As Rick says, "Scarcity is the best sales tactic." I filled out my application, and I had my interview with Rick probably a month later. Although I thought the interview went pretty well, Rick's feedback was that while I seemed like a pretty sharp guy, and I definitely knew how to close a lot of loans, he couldn't coach me because my business model sucked. He told me he didn't do Internet, he didn't do leads, and he didn't do marketing. He did relationships, and that I didn't have any. His advice was to get on the CD program and listen to the CDs for six months and see if I could get into coaching then.

Anyone who knows me knows that I don't take "no" for an answer very well. So while I didn't confront Rick on that call, over the next few weeks I started basically harassing his assistant for a face-to-face meeting with him. I finally called her and said, "Hey, I'm flying out to Charlotte tomorrow. I'd like to meet with Rick. Let me know when I can get a meeting with him."

I flew out to Charlotte without having a meeting confirmed. When I landed, I called Cat and found out that I was going to be able to have dinner with Rick that night. I met Rick for dinner, and we hit it off pretty good, which resulted in him inviting me back to his house. We sat on his back patio smoking cigars until about 2 a.m. until I finally convinced the man that I was worthy to be coached. I don't know that I actually convinced him. I think he was just tired of listening to me ramble about how great I could be if he could just take me under his wing!

So I started unofficially coaching with Rick in May 2013. At that point I hadn't originated a loan since 2008, so I dusted off the old origination boots, got on the phones, and got out in front of some agents. I closed one loan the first month I coached with Rick, then 11 loans, then 13, then 11, then 12... and then I got a phone call that the company that I worked for was going bankrupt.

That's when Rick recommended a few different banks for me, and Summit Funding made the most sense to me at that time. The only problem was that they weren't yet corporately licensed in Ohio. It was October 2013, and I essentially had to go 60 days without any way to originate a loan. All the relationships I'd made based on the reputation of my previous company fell apart over those 60 days.

I started 2014 with a new bank and not really any relationships. Keep in mind, when I started coaching with Rick, I didn't know a single, solitary real estate agent. It's not that I didn't have a relationship with any agents, I legitimately did not know a single real estate agent.

So, I did what Rick told me to do, and it was everything he told me it was. Nothing was sexy, and nothing was the newest, greatest way of going out and getting mortgage business. It was all very structured, very systematic. He taught me very basic fundamentals of how to build a business. I followed Rick's direction and finished up 2014 with my biggest personal production year ever and with my biggest income year ever. Now, in 2015, I'm on pace to blow last year's numbers out of the water.

Without The CORE, without everything that Rick has taught me, without the high level of accountability that comes with The CORE, I know without a doubt that there's absolutely no way that I could have achieved anything that I have achieved. When I was first introduced to The CORE, I thought I had it together, and I thought I knew what I was doing in this business, but at the end of the day, I was just really, really good at sales.

So my biggest strength was also my biggest weakness. I knew that I could talk my way into or out of any situation that I needed to, and as a result, I was pretty slack in the rest of the areas that you need to be strong in to be a good leader. The biggest thing I've learned in The

CORE is that you cannot have success if you do not build a team around you, and you cannot effectively make the best use of that team if you're not a good leader.

What I've learned in The CORE is just: prospect, prospect, prospect; build a team; and count the money. Everyone knows the basic principles, but there's obviously a ton of moving pieces inside of that. The great thing about The CORE is that none of those pieces is extremely complicated or involves a high-level understanding of technology, social media, and marketing. It's really based on getting into relationships with the right people, leveraging those relationships to bigger relationships, identifying and building a team specific to your needs, and leading those people by example.

# Jennifer Ellison

## Lender Coach

<u>Location</u>: Santa Barbara, California

<u>Started with The CORE</u>: January 2009

*(<u>Retired from The CORE</u>: December 2014)*

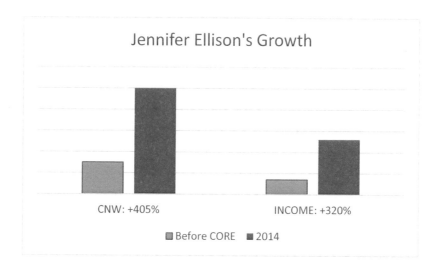

# Jennifer Ellison

In truth, I wasn't instantly drawn to The CORE. You might say I acquired a taste for its message and culture over time. When I first met Rick Ruby at a CORE Summit in Austin, Texas, in 2008, he struck me as an audacious fusion of righteous preacher meets ex-Army Drill Sargent turned raucous high school football coach. He was loud, intense, and borderline offensive. Clearly socially conservative and proud of it, he ranted on about how we were broken, out of balance, lacked focus, and in need of moral repair. He talked of relationships, systems and structure, accountability, teams and leadership, none of which were foreign concepts to me. But he approached all of it with such excitement and passion and with such simplicity and clarity. I took notice.

I had a successful 12-year run in the mortgage industry. I'd done well, had some money in the bank and was living a great life in my hometown of Santa Barbara, California. But times had changed. It was 2008 and the country was fully immersed in the mortgage meltdown. The industry had been brought to its knees by corruption, greed, dishonesty, and shame. Citizens were losing their homes to foreclosure, being deprived of pensions they'd earned after a lifetime of corporate dedication. It was a depressing time.

Somehow, Rick Ruby made it sound like a phenomenal opportunity. A gift. We were missionaries, called to transform a broken industry. I sat and I listened for two days. At a certain point I remember feeling an unfamiliar kind of panic. This insanely right wing, Christian fundamentalist, genius of a guy had moved me. He so was not my style. I think of myself as a liberal, high-minded, groovy, Southern Californian. We typically consider ourselves far too hip and intellectual to be moved by the likes of a Rick Ruby type. And yet there I was, totally moved by this man and his message. "Do your best, do the right thing, and show people you care" was the message in 2008 at The CORE convention that day. Simple, so right on, and a message many of us needed to hear.

I joined The CORE a short time after that Summit in Austin, Texas, and began piecing together a new way of running my business, and inevitably, my life. What was once muddied became clear. Complications became simple. I felt a peace I had never known.

When you recognize a new path, it's often enticing to attempt to execute too many changes all at once. It was like that for me. I made lists of changes I was going to make: hiring people to help with the mundane so I could learn to sell, creating simple structure from the chaos that shrouded my business practice, too many appointments with the wrong people, none of whom would really help me grow…But the truth was that with all the overwhelm, I felt energized again. I woke up wanting to go to work and loving my time there. I was accountable to a coach who genuinely cared about my life. That was new.

Soon I began to master certain areas of business. Systems and structure felt the most natural. I hired a team. We held morning team meetings. I learned to duplicate and replicate. My earnings grew, my family flourished, and I began saving and building wealth. I learned what it meant to be tactical. If I followed a founded set of proven rules, I could predict a particular outcome. If I earned 60 leads a month, I closed 10 deals: Plenty to make it in a luxury market like Santa Barbara.

While The CORE provided me with a proven prescription for running a business, the most important teachings I learned had little to do with business at all. It came from a deeper understanding of myself. Sometime during my first three years as a CORE student Rick Ruby gave me a homework assignment to watch a movie called Coach Carter. There is a line in the movie that I have listened to probably 50 times and can recite if asked to. I keep the written version of it next to my bed, and they are the closest holy words in my life:

"Our deepest fear is not that we are inadequate. Our deepest fear is that we are powerful beyond measure. It is our light, not our darkness, that most frightens us. Your playing small does not serve the world. There is nothing enlightened about shrinking so that other people won't feel insecure around you. We were all meant to shine as children do. It's not just in some of us. It's in everyone. As we let our own light shine, we unconsciously give other people permission to do the same. As we are liberated from our own fear, our liberation automatically liberates others."

In 2013 after six years of being coached, I became a CORE coach. I was moved to do so by the spirit embodied by those words. The CORE helped me find my own magnificence in both business and in life. It became time to "pay it forward." Today I enthusiastically coach nine students every other week. We struggle together, but always with the full conviction of or passion to be great human beings, leaders and business people.

# Jim Bass
## Realtor Coach

## Location: Ijamsville, Maryland
## Started with The CORE: July 2009

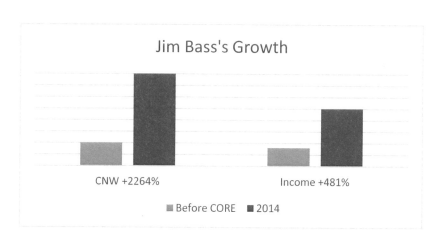

# Jim Bass

I sold my electrical contracting business in 1993 because I was tired of managing people. I told my father I was investing in a real estate brokerage business "limited service model" while I went back to school to figure out what I was supposed to do with my life.

He said, "While you're figuring it out, come sell my house."

I told him I really wasn't doing that; I was only investing while I went back to school.

He said, "While you are investing, come sell my house…"

I said, "Yes, sir!"

A friend of mine saw my father's house for sale and asked me to sell his home and help him build another.

I told him the same, "I'm not really doing this."

He said, "Okay, while you not really doing this, come sell my house."

I interviewed a couple "full-service" brokers and hung my real estate license with the #1 company in the mid-Atlantic region. I asked the older, more established agents what software they used. They laughed and pointed to the shoeboxes with 3 x 5 index cards (true story). Now remember, this is pre-cell phone, pre-lockbox, and pre-MLS. Consumers had to come to our office and look at a book of properties. I would then drive to the other real estate offices to get keys, show the properties, and return the keys to the brokerage offices.

I was constantly told by the older agents, "We don't do things that way," but ads made sense to me and people responded to the ads, so I continued to do it.

I was the guy that turned on the lights and started the coffee pot at 6:30 a.m. and turned off the coffee pot and lights at 10:30 p.m., pretty much seven days a week. I took all the floor duty I could get, and I quickly became the go-to guy if anyone needed coverage. I spent half my day generating leads on floor duty and half my day selling.

My manager informed me that I had to attend our company's annual conference. Even though I didn't have time, I obliged out of respect. Much to my shock, I was awarded Rookie of the Year for Maryland and DC (shock, because I still really did not know what I was doing).

If people wanted to see homes tomorrow, I would make a dry run the day before so that I could speak intelligently about price, bedrooms, and bathrooms for when we passed other real estate signs on the way to the homes they wanted to see.

After maintaining this pace for three years, I began to get tired and fat. I lost sight of what was most important: my faith, my family, and my health. I convinced myself that my children were too young to know I wasn't there, I left my wife to fend for herself, and allowed my very fit physique to be hidden by "fast food" fat. Now, the persona was that I had it all going on, taking care of my immediate and extended family, being seen at church and social gatherings. But I was giving my family "what was left of me, instead of the best of me" and becoming a shell of a man.

I would just work faster and harder, start my days earlier, usually at 4 a.m., so I could be present for breakfast at 8 a.m., run all day, appear at a few dinners, and then run into the night. It was all work, and I sold a lot of homes because I got addicted to the adrenaline.

It was about that time I met a man named Joe Stumpf from By Referral Only. He was the first business man I had ever met that spoke about God and business in the same breath. He also introduced a new concept where I was not constantly reinventing my business after every transaction: the "Referral Centric Business." He introduced me to Michael Gerber, author of the best-selling book "The E-Myth" (The Entrepreneurial Myth), and later to some great people who eventually changed my life: Rick Ruby, Todd Scrima, and Reeta Casey.

After becoming inspired by "The E-Myth," I immediately went back to my office and mapped out a seven-person team, which was kind of funny because at that time I only had a part-time assistant, so I was wearing 6 ½ "job" hats. But I had a plan to grow, and as my business continued to reach new levels, I would take off another hat and hand off the job with checklists for that position to the new team member so that I could maintain a balanced life with reasonable work hours.

So bigger was better: First I was at $3 million, then $5.5 million, then $8.2 million. I was continually top ranking for units in volume in the region and nation, When I reached $30 million, I realized the franchise I was affiliated with did not know how to charge the brokerage fee for teams, and it became cost prohibitive for me to maintain a team. To maintain profitability, I would have to either work more hours with fewer real estate agents or leave the franchise.

I told my wife, "If we leave the franchise and start our own brokerage, we could do 18 fewer transactions per year and still make the same money without having to pay all the franchise fees."

So in 2002, I partnered with another top-producing team to create Real Estate Teams brokerage. We bought the mayor's house, which was a center hall rancher connected to his mother-in-law's house for a total of about 10,000 square feet, converted all the garages, bedrooms and living space to offices, then added a 2,000 square foot addition, which gave us a total of 41 offices and five conference rooms.

During this time there was also talk of a new opportunity: "bundled services of real estate, mortgage and title" on the streets, and because we knew nothing about the inner workings of a mortgage company, my wife and I joined our friends, Rick, Todd, and Reeta at The CORE for their real estate and mortgage coaching program. I was ready to set the world on fire.

The structure they helped me implement into my life, my personal production team, and my companies was amazing. We implemented some much-needed job contracts, operations manuals, daily team meetings, sales training, sales skills, created productive work environments, and most importantly high quality leadership. It was also during this time that my coaches began to highlight how ill-prepared I was for the amount of time and attention that was required to successfully run several businesses.

After 2 ½ years and with the increasing amounts of demand for my time, I felt I had learned all I needed to learn, but I'll never forget my last coaching call in June 2004. Todd told me, "Leadership isn't a destination; it's a journey, and we never stop working at it." I didn't truly understand the magnitude of that statement for several years.

The thought was, "We will build it and they will come," because of the agent-centric business model, and come they did. We grew from 28 agents to 367 agents with three branch offices within the first 20 months of opening the doors. As a company we quickly took over the #1 market share, and even during all that explosive growth, my wife and I grew our personal team production from 127 sales to 181 within the first year of a new real estate brokerage that no one had ever heard of.

Because the company was in such high demand, we had other great real estate teams. They could not join us without office space, so we acquired a failed commercial project in the heart of downtown. It was dirt cheap, and we also bought the plans for 100,000 square-foot mixed-use building, and began the journey of commercial development. This quickly became a full-time job because we were building out 15,000 square feet of personal office space for our affiliated businesses. I fell back to my old ways of working faster, harder, and longer hours, again telling myself it would be short-term pain for long-term gain, especially since I leveraged our home and all of our money. Failure was not an option.

Fortunately I had grown a mega team of 15 agents doing nearly $50 million in production so that I could focus on my other projects. But, you guessed, it in the middle of this major undertaking, the great recession of 2008 hit. We had 71 reservations for office space, yet only 17 agents showed up to rent space. So I quickly began trying to right-size our office space, like every other commercial landlord in town. I jumped into the world of short sales because that was all selling, again requiring way too much time for limited results.

Fearing for my financial future, I reached out to my friends at The CORE and asked them what it looked like out their window because it didn't look so good out mine. Rick said, "You need to come back into the coaching program and we will fix it."

What I now know is that it's not about what I learn, it is about what I do on a daily basis, and even as disciplined as I am, I do it a whole lot better when someone else is watching. The CORE's motto of "Profitability Through Accountability" is my reality. I soon returned to The CORE, and I was able to right-size my operations and create better profits. My journey with The CORE has allowed me to increase my net worth from $300,000 to more than $3,000,000, lead a personal production team to $30 million in sales annually with profits higher than $50 million in sales volume. The CORE has taught me how to better lead my companies, manage people, and network to success.

I am known for "thinking outside the box," and my success is largely due to leveraging and managing people, industry networking, and being a skilled negotiator. My personal production team averages $30,000,000 in sales volume per year while I work fewer than 25 hours in my personal production team. I now pride myself in balancing successful business, which allows me to never miss a family breakfast, dinner, or extracurricular event. I have been happily married for 27 years and have three beautiful children: Brittany, 24, Mariah, 19 and Christian, 8.

I have been a speaker and panelist for several other real estate organizations but none, that I'm aware, requires everyone, from the owners to the coaches, to be high-producing practitioners. I'm on the street just like you, I compete for listing presentations, and I am face-to-face with clients and businesses asking for their referrals.

I would not be where I am today without The CORE, Rick, Todd, Reeta, Britt, and CORE Staff. The love and learning from the other world-class coaches is guaranteed to improve your life, just like it did mine. They have coached and mentored me, shared their accomplishments, failures, and successes. Since I have become a CORE coach, I am dedicated more than ever to "Improving Lives" and helping others avoid my pitfalls along the way. Every day I try to set an example of how to balance a successful real estate business while raising a family and most of all, ENJOYING being fully present with my family. Yes, there was a time when my family got "what's left of me," instead of "the best of me," but now I can consistently give them my best.

I have all the CORE systems in place, and even when the economy tanked in 2008, I maintained a steady, successful real estate practice. My business is 93% repeat referral business. And with numbers like that, we are doing it right! Jim Bass Group, Real Estate Teams is on track to have one of our best years ever.

# Jane Floyd
## Lender Coach

### Location: Tampa, Florida
### Started with The CORE: January 2011

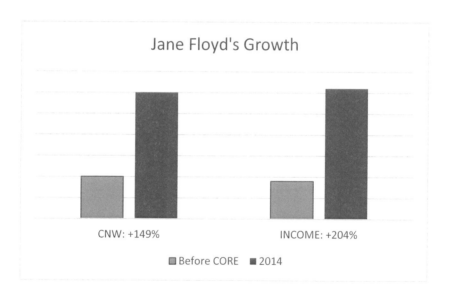

Jane Floyd's Growth

CNW: +149%          INCOME: +204%

■ Before CORE   ■ 2014

# Jane Floyd

In the fall of 2010 I accidently stumbled into a break out session of a "free" event in Orlando, Florida, and little did I know that my life was about to take a drastic change. I listened to Rick Ruby scream at a room of loan officers, and right then I knew that The CORE was exactly where I needed to be. After 24 years in the business, going through ups and downs, I was accepted into coaching in January of 2011 and have only experienced continual growth since.

Recently I was asked the question: Who is the best leader you know? The answer is Rick Ruby. I am amazed with the way that The CORE is run. Everything is tactical, thought out, and accounted for. Rick has built a team of coaches that are literally the best loan officers in the entire nation. What really stood out to me was the accountability. Nothing falls through the cracks with Rick, ever. Rick walks his walk and talks his talk. Although he sometimes has "no filter," it is truly because he wants everyone to "be the best they can be." He genuinely cares for each and every student and employee of his.

Todd Scrima and Reeta Casey are his partners for a reason. They want everyone to reach their greatest potential and experience a well-balanced, successful life, just like they have. When I first joined The CORE, I was in a crippling financial situation that had me stagnant in my career. I was to the point of moving out of my dream home and couldn't see any other options. After two of the most challenging and financially devastating years of my life, Todd Scrima gave me the confidence and the guidance to determine where I wanted my business to go. In the first two years after being accepted into coaching I doubled my income. After three years I increased another 25%. This year I am experiencing another consistent increase in my business. I was honored to be asked to be a coach and so grateful to work for such a top-notch organization like The CORE.

After my first three years in The CORE and from the direction of Rick, I knew that I needed to make yet another major change. For 22 years I had been a broker and owned my own company, but now it was time to take the next step: joining a correspondent lender. I had flown all over the country interviewing with companies trying to find the perfect fit. Then Rick Ruby introduced me to David Silverman, CEO of NFM Lending.

Now I am with NFM Lending, and I couldn't be more thrilled. I am excited with the opportunity that NFM has provided me for expansion and growth. Since joining The CORE, not only have I grown personally, but the entire culture of my office has changed. Although I have always been extremely passionate and driven, being aligned with The CORE has given me the leadership skills to build an incredible, like-minded team. Everyone is now extremely driven to see growth in our branch. Without The CORE, I would be in the same place I was back in 2010. It really is amazing to see how far I have come!

I am truly blessed!

# Jeremy Forcier
## Lender

**Location**: Petaluma, California

**Started with The CORE**: January 2011

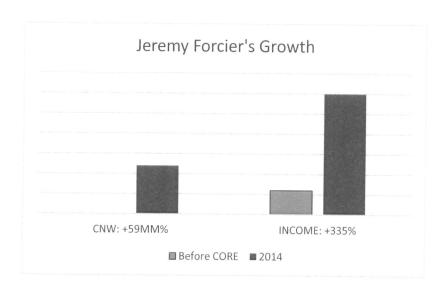

Jeremy Forcier's Growth

CNW: +59MM%    INCOME: +335%

■ Before CORE   ■ 2014

# Jeremy Forcier

I started The CORE about five years ago, and at the time, I was completely broken, a complete mess, and they helped me fix it. When I first got in The CORE, I was touted as a national speaker, as this rookie young gun hot shot. I was flown around to do massive talks about my processes and systems. I was doing between $50 and $60 million per year for production.

But while I was doing all those units, the reality was I had no money. I had a problem living outside of my means. I was making more than $275,000 a year, but I was living like I was making $1 million a year. I was $250,000 in debt, from both credit cards and tax liens. I wasn't managing my relationships right, especially my marriage. I was working 70 hours a week, and I had no team. It was a big, big, big problem.

When I joined The CORE, the first thing I learned was that I had to let my big unhealthy ego go. I needed to learn to surrender to a system. When I first tried – and tried is the key word – to join The CORE, Rick Ruby told me:

"You have to talk to your wife, and she has to sign off on this because you have completely made it so that she doesn't trust you anymore."

I said, "No problem!"

So I went to my wife, and I said, "I went to this great event, the Summit, and this is going to fix my business.

I'm going to surrender to the process, and it's going to be fantastic for our family."

I was so disconnected from my relationship that I was sure she would say yes.

I was completely wrong.

She said, "Absolutely not. You've created all this financial burden for us already, and sorry, it's a no go."

The old Jeremy would have just given The CORE my American Express card without telling my wife and done it anyway. But being around all these successful, transparent people: Rick, Todd, and all the students that I had met, I just couldn't do that. I couldn't lie anymore. I wanted to be an authentic person.

So I called Rick Ruby, and I remember I left this message: "Rick, man I would love to part of this CORE thing, but my wife just is not buying into it. She doesn't want me paying $2,000 a month when we're $276,000 in the hole and we just lost a house. She's really upset with me. I've got to work on this relationship."

I thought that was that. I said I was going to do the CDs, and in six months go to the Summit and try it again.

I got a call from Rick Ruby and he said, "My God, Jeremy! That must have been the first time you told the truth in the last four years. I'm so proud of you!"

I was really taken back by this voicemail. What did he mean?

And then he offered to earn my business.

It was just the craziest thing. I mean I get choked up even talking about it. Someone who I had only known casually for two months believed in me that much and was willing to help me out.

Rick coached me on the side for free, pro bono, for 30 minutes every two weeks. It was strictly about my budget and my wife. I paid off more than $50,000 in debt in that first six months. By the time I went back to the

Summit, my wife said, "All right. This looks like the real deal." I signed up, and the rest is history.

I went from making $276,000 when I started to $550,000 in the first year. Over the last five years, my numbers have kept climbing: $750,000, then $988,000, to $1.2 million in 2014. Right now I'm on track to make $1.4 million in 2015. I started with $276,000 in debt, and I now have $600,000 in the bank. But what's even better is that my relationship with my wife is the best it's ever been.

I went from a team of me and one assistant when I started with The CORE to a team of five right now, and according to Rick, I'm still understaffed. I have a problem hiring, and I'm always working on that.

The coolest thing about this journey for me has been that I know I'm never going to be perfect, and that's okay. I've learned to always be honestly authentic, to give 100 percent, to really care about other people, and to always be in love with my business. I'm constantly reminded of those things, and to be around such an incredible group of originators and coaches in the industry is truly a blessing. So I'm broken, and I always will be, but The CORE is always there to help take me to the next level and focus on all the right things.

Life is good.

# Kristy Cantleberry

**Realtor**

**Location:** Grand Blanc, Michigan

**Started with The CORE:** January 2014

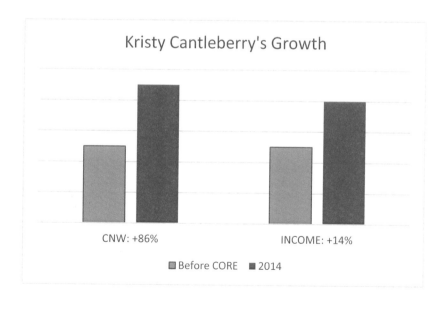

# Kristy Cantleberry

You should do something every day that scares you. I joined The CORE.

I started in real estate in 1998 in a small Michigan market after answering an ad for real estate agents in a local newspaper. I thought, "I can do that; how hard can it be?" Then the fun began. I never imagined that selling houses would turn into such a business. I was just doing this for "fun."

Since 1998, I have hired two real estate coaching firms that have helped me grow my business. I am now being coached by The CORE, and this program is quite different from anything I have ever been involved in. I was invited to meet Rick Ruby in person at his office because someone thought we might be a good fit. Let me tell you, I left the meeting not liking him! He challenged my every sentence and wouldn't even listen to me. He followed me out into the parking lot when I left and told me I needed to join his coaching program. Something about the challenge intrigued me, so I went to one of Rick's events and joined.

I know now that if Rick is yelling, it is because he cares. He knows every one of his clients personally and is always available to talk. Unlike the other coaching programs I was involved with, The CORE teaches you about profit and loss and how to build relationships. My industry is always pushing for more ads, billboards, radio, buying leads, etc. The bleeding never stops. I was spending so much money to increase my sales but my bottom line profit needed a lot of work.

I have been involved with The CORE for two semesters now, and I agreed to surrender early. The CORE program always assigns you a coach that is producing at a level above you. Kendra Cooke, who has been my coach for both semesters, taught me that Rome was not built in a day. It takes consistent hard work to build a winning team. We work on increasing our bottom line profit and knowing where our business is coming from. I actually reduced my marketing dollars and saw my business increase. The main thing I have learned is that you have to know your numbers. It took me a long time to grasp this, but once I got it, I started making better business decisions.

My team and I produce about $30 million in sales each year, and I have always increased my business each year, but I still did not know how to run one. By being involved in The CORE, it's being held accountable for everything you do that truly takes you to the next level. The people you are surrounded by are all down to earth and willing to help with anything you need. They all go through the same hiccups each day that we all face in this business. This company truly cares and does everything they say that they will do. I am certain that they will help me create the future that I am planning for. Don't get me wrong, I didn't say it would be easy, but being surrounded with this group pushes me to be my best.

Rick always tells me: "We will always be broken." Being in a room full of broken people makes me realize I love being broken. If you are searching for who you were meant to be in life, this program will get you there. Remember, it has to start with YOU, but having the right people to help makes it a lot easier.

# Scott Forman

## Lender Coach

### Location: Montvale, New Jersey

### Started with The CORE: January 2011

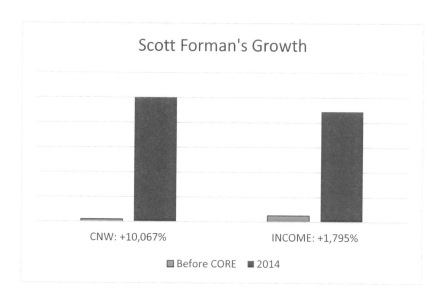

# Scott Forman

I started my career in the mortgage banking industry during the great run-up in the housing market. Interest rates were high, but sentiment was flying even higher, and mortgage companies popped up everywhere. After the financial crisis decimated the housing market, and despite unprecedented low rates, it became far more competitive to truly create a lasting and sustainable business in the mortgage industry.

Like most loan originators, I didn't grow up thinking I was going to be a mortgage banker – it wasn't even on my top 10 list of careers I wanted to pursue. The prospect of having an income that was only limited by my initiative and achievement was intriguing, and as a life-long hard worker, I saw no reason to be limited by the "ceiling" a traditional salary offered.

On my first day in the mortgage industry, I met with the branch manager, very excited to start my training in this new field. The manager showed me to my new cubicle, where there was a telephone, a computer, and two old phone books.

He said, "Call a lot of people and you'll do fine."

I'm a self-starter by nature, but I had expected a more formalized training. In the early days, I would go to staff meetings and hear terms like PITI and 15/30 balloon mortgage and scurry back to my cubicle to Google them, writing in my composite notebook for future reference. I never understood why there wasn't more training.

Over my first few years in the mortgage industry, I successfully grew all on my own. I was told that to be successful you had to make a lot of phone calls, so I made 75 phone calls a day. I did open houses on Saturday and Sunday, broker open's on Tuesday, and real estate tours on Thursday. I would meet with a client, then rush to see my son's little league game, and then would be on the phone or the computer the rest of the night. I was always taught that if I wanted to make more money, I had to work more hours, so I was working 80 hours a week. With my production increasing month over month, the owner of the company promoted me to branch manager after only one year. I kept up that growth pace for many years. The success was great, but I was concerned that working these excessive hours, while positive financially, would be a strain on my family life.

With all of the phone calls, all of the appointments, and all of the hours I was working, I felt that I had reached a plateau where my production vacillated between good and mediocre in subsequent years. The growth was organic, and while my business expanded and sometimes contracted, I always blamed the down years on the market, the weather, or rates. I was always confident that I had charted the best course forward. More importantly, I felt that my time was being well-spent and that I operated at or near peak efficiency.

*I was very wrong.*

I have always been a student of the mortgage business, going to seminars and reading books from anyone that would offer advice. I came to the realization that most of these people that were giving their advice, in fact, had not originated a mortgage in over 10 years. How were they going to help me in my market today?

In 2010, my friend Bill called me, very excited, and told me about this coaching organization that was holding a two-day conference in California. He said the conference sold out fast, that I had to let him know if I wanted to go and he would sign us up right away. I did some quick research and signed up for the two-day event. Three months later I was on my way to my first Summit.

Not knowing what to expect, and feeling a little nervous, I walked into the conference room sat down. I saw Rick Ruby for the first time and turned to Bill and said, "Who is that guy up on stage yelling and screaming?" Rick started off by welcoming everyone with a passion that I have never seen before. Then that passion turned to yelling and telling everyone that their business model was "broken," we all worked too many hours and didn't work smart. I'm from New York, so I felt right at home.

I met a lot of people that had the same frustrations as I did, working exorbitant hours, staying on their cell phones until 9 or 10 o'clock at night. Over the next two days, I was in classes and learned more tactical training than I had in all of my past years in the mortgage industry put together. When the Summit was over, like everyone else, I was extremely eager to get accepted into The CORE program. I signed my letter of intent and went back home.

I walked into my office on Monday full of excitement and eager to make major changes in my office. Consequently, I returned to an unresolved closing issue from the previous week, an appraisal that was below the value that we needed to make a loan work. I went back to my old habits without making any of the changes I had just been taught.

I kept thinking that I would begin to implement those things I learned from the Summit next week. That went on for weeks before I even changed one thing. Ninety-nine percent of the changes I was eager to make never were implemented. I was excited about the possibility of being coached, but first I had to go home to my wife and explain that I wanted to join this elite coaching organization, and that the cost was $2,000 per month. She was used to me spending hundreds of dollars on books, tapes and CDs from industry "experts" and would ask me, "How much are you really getting out of these?" I would say that I was only looking for something to make me better. Now I was saying that I want to spend $2,000 each month! Considering the fact that I had been married for more than 30 years, you would think this would have been easier, but I felt like my teenage self telling my mother, "I really need a car to go to school so I can study more in the library." My wife reluctantly agreed (so had my mother about the car; I guess I was meant to be in sales).

The next week I received a call from one of Rick's assistants to schedule my interview call. They told me to fax in my previous year's tax return and be prepared to answer a list of questions. I was very intrigued that that Rick himself would be calling.

The time came for my call with Rick, and I was uncharacteristically nervous. His call came in exactly when scheduled. I was excited to tell him the successes that I had had and that I was "thinking about joining The CORE" because I believed I needed a little tweaking in my business model. He asked me very pointed questions on my business and business activities. By the time our phone conversation was over, I found myself almost begging to be accepted into the program, realizing that my business model did not need tweaking – it was absolutely BROKEN. He asked me if I was committed to being open to change and had the ability to be coachable. I told him yes!

I received a call the next week telling me that I had been accepted into the program. January rolled around, and I wasn't really sure what to expect from my first semester. On Rick's initial call with me, he asked me if I was committed to being coached and would I be a good student. I told him yes, however, that this was a harder task than I had anticipated. I had done things "my way" for 20 years and thought that I would make subtle changes a little at a time. I had a great first coach who explained what was expected of me.

I figured, "A few forms? This is all it takes?"

I started making some changes. My first task was to see 15 people face to face and have 60 conversations per week. No sweat! The first few weeks I saw eight or so people per week, and I rationalized to myself that I was on the phone trying to get my 60 calls and that I would just make up my face to face appointments the following week. The following week would come, and I would make 15 appointments, but only end up seeing 12 and to my frustration, I only had 44 calls on my Greatness Tracker.

I had to miss my next coaching call because I had to reschedule a Real estate agent lunch appointment. I figured this was an acceptable excuse for missing my coaching call. My coach knew how hard I was working and that this was a business appointment. On my next coaching call, my coach fined me for missing the call. I was starting to get what they meant by "accountability." I kept thinking back to when I played football and my coach fined me when I missed a block and made me run laps. This was going to take some real getting used to now that I had somebody watching my business activities every day, week, month.

I must have been putting in 75 hours a week. My business was still a mess, but I couldn't see it at the time. I was starting to get frustrated with my inability to consistently fill up my Greatness Tracker and keep track of my leads and their sources. I also did not realize that Rick, Todd, and Reeta keep track of every student's work and their progress.

After two months in The CORE, I was sitting in my office and I got a call on my cell phone from Rick Ruby. I thought he must have seen how hard I was working and wanted to give me a pep talk. I was excited to pick up the call and hear what Rick had to say, until I actually answered.

Rick said, "Although we like you, this is going to have to be your first and last semester with us."

He went on to say that they didn't feel I was following instructions well and my effort to change was not there. More importantly, he said he didn't think I was coachable. I was shocked. (I also thought, "Hey, I am paying $2,000 per month and they actually want me to leave the program?")

I felt this immediate wave of panic come over me and pleaded with Rick that I was a little stubborn and not used to a lot of change but if he gave me one more chance, I would follow The CORE structure 100%. One thing I learned about Rick over the years was that he really does not want to give up on any of his students and that even though there is a long waiting list to get into the program, if you have the will and desire, he will not let you fall. This was my first "ah-ha" moment and the first of many to come.

With a renewed sense of commitment and focus, I attacked my Greatness Tracker. My goal was to hit all my numbers on all of my forms. Of course, that was easier said than done. However, my numbers slowly began to rise. By the fourth month, I saw an increase in my closings. Historically, I had had the typical rollercoaster career: one month good with closings and the next month a poor amount of closings. I found that this was now starting to level off, and I steadily had consistent good closing months. Looking back, it was so simple to see that because I was forced to keep up my intense level of prospecting while managing my current closings, my rollercoaster income began to level off and was doing so at a higher level.

The next semester came, and I was eager to see who my next coach was going to be. I received the e-mail with the new coaching calendar and quickly looked to the bottom to find that my new coach was Rick Ruby.

Many thoughts rushed through my head, but panic was the only one I can remember. The semester started out right from the beginning with Rick pushing us to do things that I not only had never thought to do, but quite frankly, never had the guts to do.

With my desire to never disappoint this man who had given me a second chance to stay in this program, I did everything he asked me to do. I made appointments with five brand new Real estate agents every week, along with attorneys, title companies, etc. He gave me an assignment to make an appointment with two new builders.

I told him, "This is New York. It is already built up and there are no builders around here."

In typical Rick form, he said, "I don't care. Find two!"

Not wanting to disappoint, I actually found two and met with them. One of them just had put up a condo complex, and the bank that they were using to finance the construction was doing a poor job with the individual loans for the units. I became the primary lender for the rest of the 62 unsold units. Needless to say, I have never questioned Rick's assignments again.

My next coach taught me the mechanics of the "sale" and the structure of a sales call. By the time the semester was over, I was in a great routine, balancing my prospecting activities with maintaining my pipeline and closing ratio. My income had doubled, and things were working well.

I was still working too many hours when my next semester rolled around. My next coach was Todd Scrima, and he showed me how to build my team, give them definitive job duties, and most importantly, create accountability so I did not have to micro manage, which enabled me to prospect even more than I had been.

My income has risen 10 times my original gross, and my saving has gone from virtually nothing to millions. When Rick asked us to write down our journey through The CORE, I was reluctant to start, as I thought, "How much do I really have to say?" But once I started writing this, I realized that I probably could have written my own book.

The CORE is not just teaching you how to be a great income producer, but to be a great saver of your money and a better leader. The thing that people don't realize is that you also become a better husband, parent, and have a keen sense and desire to make other people's lives better.

# Greg Gale
## Lender Coach

## Location: Scottsdale, Arizona
## Started with The CORE: January 2011

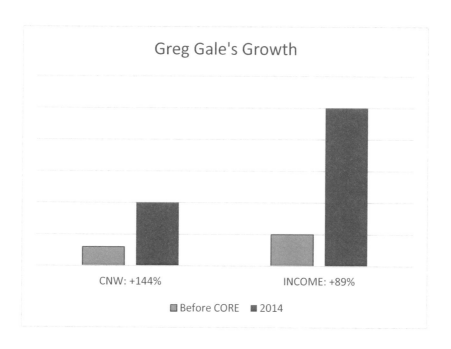

# Greg Gale

As I sit down to write about my CORE journey, it's now been six years since the passing of my mentor in the business and friend JB. I grew up in Quincy, MA, and moved to Arizona to go to school at Arizona State University. After graduating with a degree in exercise science and physiology, I was a trainer at the top health club in the Southwest, and I was running the martial arts program.

One of my first clients was a mortgage broker named Kathy. My girlfriend at the time and now wife, Katie, wanted to get into real estate. Kathy encouraged me to have Katie talk with her. They spoke, and Katie started in the mortgage industry. Over the course of a few years, she worked her way up to vice president of the company. As I was looking to change careers, Katie said there was a top producer in her office that was looking for an assistant. She felt like this was my opportunity to make a move, so I sat down with JB and within a couple weeks, I started working as JB's assistant.

At the time, JB was working from dusk 'til dawn, averaging 20 deals a month by himself. His highest month was 31. Over the next three years I sat in the same office as JB, where I absorbed as much as I possibly could. I had absolutely no loan experience when I started. JB taught me how to do loans the right way, meaning treat people how you would want to be treated, give them a good deal with GREAT service. He taught me how to have a traditional referral-based business in regards to retaining clients for life. He was amazing in regards to relationships. His phone would just ring all day long. At one point the IT guy came into our office and said there were three times as many calls going to into our office as anyone else. That didn't even count the cell phones.

My job was to keep him in his chair at all times. I would set up the files, talk to borrowers, and oversee the file pipeline. In CORE terms, I would've been the LP2/Team Captain. During my time with JB, we averaged over 40 deals per month with our largest being 56. That was with no assistants, one processor, and an assistant processor.

At that time, my job was to support JB and make sure that he was always selling, meeting with clients, and structuring loans. Once it was a deal, I would simply run with it until closing. In 2007, JB opened up his own office under the umbrella of the current brokerage. Later that year is when we realized the suffocation of the brokering world and started researching private mortgage banking. All of 2008 was a search for a new place to call home.

On September 10, 2008, JB passed away in a horrible ATV accident. We shut down the brokerage and closed out all the files at the original office. I moved to my current company, NOVA Home Loans, with my processor. I was starting from scratch. I had never originated a loan, I had never taken an application nor structured a file. I had sat with JB for more than three years, and until I started doing those things, I hadn't realized how much I had absorbed.

Here is where The CORE came into the picture. I had just lost my boss, partner, leader, mentor and friend. I knew I needed help, but had no idea where to turn besides my new company. I had signed up for a leadership conference in Mesa, Arizona. It was an all-day conference that was held about a month after JB passed. The CORE was not there, but for some reason their CDs were. I grabbed one and listened to it on the way home. It was Rick Ruby at a seminar hosted by Manesh Baxi. After listening the first time, I checked out their website and signed up for the CD program.

Right about then the market in Arizona was turning from refinance to purchase, which was perfect timing to get a CORE CD. I listened to the CDs and did everything they said. My background was martial arts, and I used to manage one of the most successful full-time martial arts schools in Arizona. I am extremely disciplined and simply did what the CDs told me to do. My highest year prior to the CORE income wise was $110,000. After one year on the CD program, I was at $229,000. Within four months, I had hired an assistant. My volume grew, and then that person left. I hired another one, and shortly thereafter, that person left as well.

Looking back now I realize I was horrible at interviewing, checking references, personality profiling, etc. The CORE has taught me invaluable lessons on recruiting talent and retaining them as well. After a year on CDs, I went to my first Summit. WOW! Talk about drinking from the fire hose. That was a lot of information. I implemented quite a bit, but not as much as if I had a live coach looking at my business all the time – not that I knew that at the time. That year, my income went over $300,000. I went to my second Summit and then applied to be coached.

My first assignment was to track my hours. At the time I had one assistant, and I was working close to 83 hours per week. I would leave work at 2 a.m. and leave a message for Travis at The CORE, since they were East Coast. I would then leave him another message at 5 a.m.

as I was on my way to the gym. At the time, it was no big deal. All my life I've worked long days, long hours and associated that with being successful. Today I measure success in different ways. My wife came to me during my first semester with The CORE and said she "felt like a single mother," and that I needed to make a change. I spoke to my coach and proceeded to hire two more people. My hours dropped to 60, which was a huge improvement, but I still needed work. Currently, I'm at 45 and will be below 40 by the end of the year.

What I really like about The CORE is that they focus on the WHOLE. We call it the Seven Wheels of Life. I've realized over the years that each of these areas affects the other. If you're struggling at home or with your health, your work will suffer. If you've saved a lot of money and feel secure, and your significant other is happy and you're in good health, then your business will thrive. It's seems simple and basic, but so many of us get caught up in work that every aspect suffers, and you don't realize it until something catastrophic happens or you get a COACH with an outside view to correct your course.

Since being coached, my income and savings has increased year over year. My team has grown to five plus me. My hours have decreased from 85 to 45. I have gone on more vacations in the last couple years and created many, many memories that my wife, Katie, and my two kids, Kai and Tatum, will have forever. These things would never have happened without The CORE's influence and impact on my life and business.

What I've enjoyed is that it is a simple process of systems, tactics, and structure that is easy to follow. Sometimes the difficult part is to surrender to these systems. Most of us naturally fight the norm and think we have a better way. On the contrary, the results are proven time and time again by the top producers at The

CORE. They lead by example and are transparent with their business. They come from a place of abundance. I look forward to many, many years with The CORE, always as a student and now as a coach. I look forward to continuing to "pay it forward."

# Shayla Gifford
## Lender Coach

## Location: Reno, Nevada
## Started with The CORE: January 2011

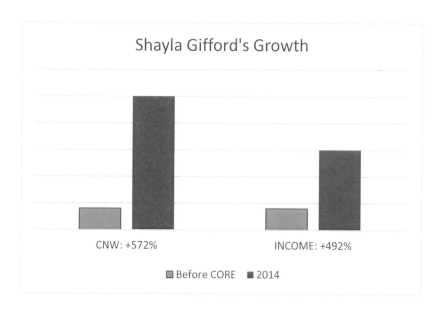

Shayla Gifford's Growth

CNW: +572%    INCOME: +492%

■ Before CORE    ■ 2014

# Shayla Gifford

Based on my avid dedication to my high school academic career and a straight "A" report card, you would have thought I would be the first one in my family to get a college degree.

Instead, I dropped out of college after my freshman year, got into sales, and today run a small mortgage operation for Guild Mortgage with 56 employees. I am 33 years old and live in Reno, Nevada. I am married to my rad husband, Galen, and together we have a 3 ½-year-old daughter, Gemma, and a 7-month-old daughter, Gwennyth.

I am a loan originator, a branch manager, a CORE training coach, a Guild Mortgage National sales coach, a mother, a wife, and a friend. I am stoked to be all of them, and most days are darn good at life.

Growing up, my parents always said "you set your own bar" and lectured me and my three siblings on the idea that we could have it all. We could be madly in love, have a great marriage with loving families, have great careers, travel the world, and have lots of fun. They continued to say, "All of this is possible if you work hard."

So I did. I have been a grinder since I was 15 years old when I played volleyball. I practiced for hours, went to camps, and sometimes fell asleep holding a volleyball in my arms. In school, I didn't just want to get an "A." I wanted 100% scores.

When I got to college and realized most of my peers were there to graduate in five years and drink as much beer as possible, I quickly realized I was an outcast. After three months in school at the University of Arizona, I answered an ad in the college newspaper and signed up to sell vitamins with a network marketing company.

I went to meetings weekly, started reading sales books, and surrounded myself with motivated people. Initially I sucked!! I had been so focused on my grades and winning at whatever sport I did, I hadn't learned great people skills, and sales was hard for me.

The summer I turned 19 I decided to move to Chicago and get coached by the top sales person in the company. He was ruthlessly tough on me, and I got results. Being a former pro hockey player, he also pounded me on hard work, swallowing my ego, and doing whatever it takes to be great.

After four years under his "Stalin-like" leadership and living in Ohio, I was ready to move home to Reno. Fortunately someone told me I would never make it in the mortgage business since I was a girl who had no experience or education. That man will never know the favor he did for me by saying I wasn't good enough.

At 23 years old in 2004, I jumped into the mortgage business as a loan officer. Immediately I fell in love. I felt I had a purpose and delivered a real benefit in helping others with their finances. I was able to apply my nerdy math addiction with my developed sales skills, and I found success immediately. In my first six years I averaged 140 loans per year and created a wonderful reputation as someone who could get things done quickly, was always available and responsive, and wouldn't be shy to tackle a tough situation. I focused primarily on refinance business and worked like a freak.

All seemed great until 2008 happened and the faucet shut off. To maintain my business in a financial crisis the only strategy I knew was to work harder.

By the end of 2009, I almost quit the business. I had just married the love of my life but was working 12 hours a day and was completely stressed to the max. Every vacation we took, whether El Salvador, Costa Rica, Mexico or Indonesia, I brought my work and the stress with me. I left Galen after three runs on perfect blue bird Sunday morning ski days to go to the office, and the worst part was I sometimes checked emails from the chairlift.

The "hard work" theory almost killed me. But, I kept telling myself, where else can a "girl with no education" go and earn this kind of living?

Thankfully, in that time when I felt lost, my world was shaken up. My company consolidated, reorganized, restructured or whatever… basically fired me and I was forced to make major changes.

I interviewed nine mortgage companies to find my "forever" home. When I found Guild Mortgage, I also found The CORE Training. I started listening to CDs with this loud, direct, tell-it-like-it-is coach, Rick Ruby. As a result, I started regaining my faith and hope in the business. I opened a branch for Guild Mortgage on May 1, 2010 and hired my first assistant, Lynette Bonnett. I also attended my first CORE Summit event 10 days later and was blown away. I had so many systems to implement in order to get my business back on track and moving forward.

I met other loan officers from around the country that were earning three and four times what I was, but also had a life and worked maybe 50 hours per week. The

CORE students I met had a plan, had systems and checklists, and a purpose to every activity they did.

I walked away saying, "If they can do it, then I can do it!" Initially, I tried to implement all of these new forms, techniques, tools, etc. by myself. I thought, why pay $2,000 per month when I can listen to CDs and figure it out?

Well, I made progress and I became pregnant! But when I came back to the Summit in November 2010, I was impatient and ready to make even more progress and faster. With a baby on the way and being the primary bread winner, it was time to step it up.

I became a level 3 student in January 2011, and two coaching calls later, I gave birth to my first daughter Gemma.

The first two years of coaching were a blur. I completely surrendered to the process and whatever I was told, I did. My income doubled the first year, and I ended the year with three team members and two loan officers in 2012. By 2013, I doubled my income again and made over $2,000,000!

To go from a two-woman branch and team closing 140 loans in 2010, to a 56-employee branch closing 492 loans personally and 1,400 as a branch in 2013 has been NUTS and a lot of fun.

This happened one day at a time, implementing one new strategy or system at a time. I have learned who to hire, how to build a team, leadership skills, creating and living a vision, how to sell, how to coach others, be authentic, save money, think big, get uncomfortable, and most importantly how to let go!!

Although earning the money, Branch of the Year Award in 2013, the president's club trips, and coaching honors have been nice, those accomplishments pale in comparison to the security I now feel.

I cherish the life I have gained! I know I will be able to have it all with skills I have learned and be able to keep my priorities straight. I am now able to work 45 hours a week or less, shut off my phone at night and be present with my husband and daughters. My vacations are now 100% work free!

Honestly, with my crazy workaholic tendencies and pre-CORE behaviors, I would probably be out of the business, divorced, or a very stressed and sad person. Fortunately, I had the guts to give this a shot and change.

The journey has just begun, and with Rick Ruby's friendship and guidance, I am now able to change the lives of others with this coaching, and my family will forever be positively impacted.

# Starling Davis
## Realtor

**Location**: Nashville, Tennessee

**Started with The CORE**: January 2009

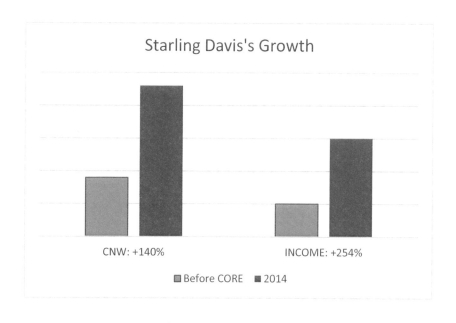

Starling Davis's Growth

CNW: +140%          INCOME: +254%

■ Before CORE   ■ 2014

# Starling Davis

I was born in a small town in Middle Tennessee and went to college in Nashville, where I earned a bachelor of science in social work. I married, had two children, and became a single parent when my children were seven months and two-and-a-half years old. I was very interested in law, and fascinated by real estate law, so I got my real estate license in 1983. I spent my first year building business from doing open houses.

In 2008, I heard about The CORE and attended my first Summit. The market was really down, and I knew I needed to find a different way to survive in the industry. I thought that Rick was way over the top and a little crazy, but fascinating. He was not the norm, but I was no longer in the normal market and needed to not only survive, but do well in the industry. The other coaches seemed strong and aggressive in a positive way and had a business formula that I wanted!

I struggled making changes and surrendering the first several years. My coaches have all been exceptional, always telling me I could do more with less effort. It took a long time for that to sink in and for me to leverage myself. I am still a work in progress and always will be!

My personal life has changed in that I have more time for my family and friends. For the most part, I do not work on Sundays anymore. My business has multiplied four times, and I look forward to my next five years, anticipating how my business will grow and change even more!

My biggest ah-ha moment was realizing that more work is not necessarily more income. Leveraging yourself with correct balance makes all the difference, *balance* being the key word.

I look forward to being the manager of my group – and only the manager – in the next five years. The CORE will help me complete the balance and enable my continued growth for my group. Someday, 15 years from now, I will complete my exit strategy. Until then, the story goes on!

# Jennifer Hernandez

## Lender Coach

**Location:** Houston, Texas

**Started with The CORE:** January 2010

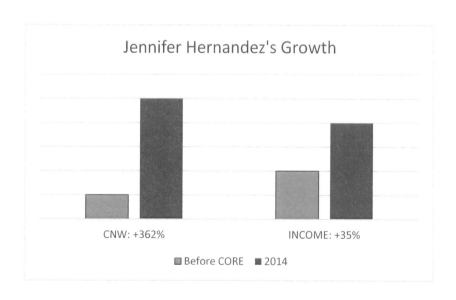

# Jennifer Hernandez

What is my story? I'm just a normal gal. Since an early age, my parents instilled in me the basics. Do what you're told. Do the right thing. Treat others like you want to be treated. Do what you promise. These principles helped me greatly during college, where I worked my way through, paying my own way 100% via student loans and working 40-plus hours a week as a waitress at Bennigan's Tavern. I sacrificed Texas A&M football games, parties with friends and sorority life, because money had to be made, and everyone knows parents visit on the weekends, and those are the tippers.

After graduation in 1994, I had an economics degree from Texas A&M, was fluent in Spanish after a recent year abroad in Mexico as an exchange student, and terrified of a 9 to 5 life. So I continued to wait tables in my hometown of Houston for nine months after graduation. I was procrastinating. In September of 1995, after a mental breakdown, I decided to work for a friend that had just started a mortgage company, Republic State Mortgage. Robert Wagnon and I had been buddies at A&M, so I thought, "This will be fun if nothing else," and I was looking for any excuse not to wait tables all weekend while 'normal' people enjoyed life.

Aside from a few college professors and my grandfather, Robert was my first true mentor. He showed me how to cold call. I remember on Fridays, if I hadn't gotten an application that week, he would say, "Call, go out, I don't care what you do, but don't come back until you have an application." He taught me the urgency of asking for the deal. Begging. So not long after I started, I remember opening the Sunday paper, which always released real estate top producers for the quarter, and calling ALL of them.

I would simply say, "You don't know me, but I'm so proud of you for your accomplishments! Congratulations on your achievement. Oh by the way, I am hosting a broker open house at 123 Smith Street Tuesday. Four bedroom, a pool, for $250K. You should come in case you have a buyer!" That was the start of my real estate agent pipeline.

Robert's mentorship also gets credit for my 'cheesy' marketing events title. He was the king of cheese: gifting, random acts of kindness, random events. He would call five agents on a Friday, give them ten minutes to clear their day, and take them across the state line to gamble all afternoon. They loved him. I was always along for the ride. They began to know me, like me, and send me deals.

Within three years, I was making over $200,000 a year, and was well known in the upper-end Houston real estate circles, despite my young age of 27. I worked late, I worked weekends, and most importantly, if I made a promise, it happened. Also, I was known for doing the impossible. Persistency is my mojo. I don't take "no" for an answer – just ask my husband!

Fast forward to 2009. My production had been stalled for three years at $50 million, with an average of 12 loans a month, which was successful for any loan officer, except I was broke. I had successfully hidden our finances from my husband for 11 years of our marriage. I paid the bills. My motto of "If you need more money, just work another shift" from my waitressing days was working in the mortgage industry, too! If I needed more money, I just closed a few more loans! This worked for a while, until a few bad decisions (like starting a net branch for my mentor of 11 years, Republic State Mortgage) proved to be a horrible idea. I'm not a manager. I'm a producer. I love people! My Disc Test 'I' score is off the charts! So after four years of income going backwards, I got out, and was on the way up again, but after accumulation of a few years of spending more than I made, I was $106,000 in debt. And my husband didn't know about it. Uh oh.

So in 2009 I met some guy named Rick Ruby, thanks to Dixie Sanders, a colleague at the time. She held a small forum for our company loan officers, and he showed up. He asked me my average yield spread, and I proudly said 1.0%. He told me my pricing sucked and that I was giving Nordstrom service for Wal-Mart pricing. He also told me that I spent too much money. So I changed my ways, and the very NEXT day, put a line in the sand, and did business with no one for less than 1.5%. An immediate raise!

By the time I attended my first Summit in November 2009, my debt was $0, and I was ready to get more from this guy that had already changed my ways. I had no idea what this 'Summit' was about, but I trusted my instinct and flew to Orlando for three days. Coaching afterwards was a no brainer for me. I know myself well enough to know that discipline is my weakest link, and I needed someone to tell me what to do. So I signed in January 2010, and my first coach was Josh Sigman.

The last five years has been life changing to say the least. In the first two years, I saved $800,000 and went from an income of $500,000 to $950,000. Rick asked me to be a coach, and I said YES! The best part about being a coach? To see Rick, Todd, and Reeta in action, leading our team, is truly an amazing experience. Our "daily team meetings" at the Summit, the way the coaches are led each week with our meetings, are EXACTLY what they teach us. Also the friendships with the coaches, and what I learn from each of them is amazing.

The CORE has taught me discipline, structure, leadership, time management, and keeping it SIMPLE. Five years ago, The CORE gave me purpose and vision at a time when I had absolutely none. I am so thankful that these people came into my life! The CORE is now part of the legacy that I am creating. When God decides my time has come, the people whose lives I have affected through friendship, coaching, mentorship, leadership, and love, will remember that I was a good soldier, a giver, loved to mentor, always shared ideas (i.e. talking too much), always time blocking, and last but not least, a cheesy event gal who loved people and had too many relationships. I can handle that.

# Chris Haynes
## Lender Coach

## Location: Mt. Juliet, Tennessee
## Started with The CORE: July 2011

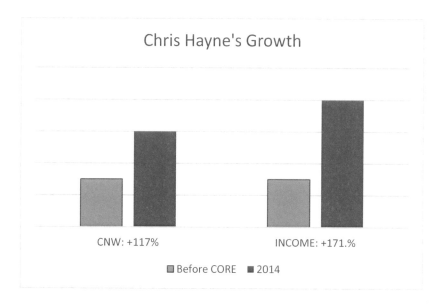

Chris Hayne's Growth

CNW: +117%   INCOME: +171.%

■ Before CORE   ■ 2014

# Chris Haynes

I started in the mortgage industry in July 2004. I had graduated from college in May 2003 and gotten married to Melissa in August of that same year. I sold cars for about seven months while Melissa finished school to become a nurse. My wife and I moved to Nashville, Tennessee, in June 2004. Melissa was working as a nurse, and I had big plans for my career in the mortgage business!

My friend, Haynes Johnson, had helped me get a job with Peoples Home Equity Inc., a Nashville-based mortgage broker. I started in an office with four other loan officers and one processor. I had no idea what I was doing! Luckily my branch manager and friend both encouraged me to go after the purchase market by building relationships with real estate agents. I focused on the FSBO market and helping FSBO's sell their homes, and that helped me meet Real estate agents and buyers along the way. In my first full month I closed two loans!

I knew from day one that I wanted to be my own boss by either owning my own mortgage company or by having my own branch. With that in mind, I continued to grow my business by referrals of friends, family and Real estate agents I had met. In 2005, my brother Clint graduated from college and moved to Nashville to work with us. I continued to work hard every day and took great pride in always answering my phone. Back then we basically originated and processed our own files. We were the only point of contact for the client and had to gather conditions etc. for the loan to get to closing.

In 2006 my 1099 topped $100,000 and I thought I had made it! As we went along, our volume grew to the point where in 2008 I was ready to make the leap and open my own branch. Clint joined me, and we opened up a two-office-space branch of PHE. We were in an office building where you could rent as few or as many spaces as you wanted. This kept my overhead low and would allow me to get my feet wet running a branch. I actually shared my 12 x 12 office with a processor for a little while. Looking back, it was crazy! Little did I know that the financial markets were about to take a dive in late 2008. We worked through that very trying time in our industry, and I am thankful and feel blessed to have been with a company that made it through the "meltdown."

We moved our branch to Mount Juliet, Tennessee, in January 2010 and finally had some extra space to be able to grow. We moved in with a couple of my best friends and clients, who were Real estate agents, and shared the space. It was also in 2010 when I really got interested in growing my business. At that time we met our awesome processor, Aly, who is with us to this day. I got a call from Travis at The CORE who signed me up for The CORE's CD program. I also attended a Lunch & Learn put on by one of the CORE coaches later that year and signed up for the May 2011 Summit. Just the CDs alone changed and grew my business. In 2010 I closed about 70 loans and made just over $200,000.

2011 got off to a slow start for us, so when we got to the Summit I was ready to learn. The first day my brother and I whipped up on Rick pretty good in the basketball game – that was just fun. Once the Summit began, I remember being a little bit overwhelmed with all the things I was learning from all these superstars on stage, and at the same time I was also surprised by how "real" these superstars seemed. They did not come off as larger than life or doing anything so extraordinary that I could not copy them and have great results too.

That Summit was awesome, and during the final presentation they asked us to fill out a form to request an interview to be coached. I remember sitting there and actually was not sure if I would fill it out or not. I had made over $200,000 and I thought that the price tag of $2,000/month (at that time) was pretty steep. I thought hard, but I told myself it was worth the risk, and I filled out the form. Two weeks later Rick Ruby called me, and I was in. Now the work was about to begin.

The first semester is HARD! The forms were new and difficult. But, I knew what I had signed up for, and I was not going to fail. I made the 30 Real estate agent calls on Mondays, every single Monday. It took about a month of practice, but I started filling up my Greatness Tracker each week. Jim Reed was my coach, and he changed the course of my business. He told me I needed to hire a loan partner.

I thought, "No way! I have a great processor! What do I need more overhead for?"

I had not bought in to the team idea yet. We did hire another person to start helping with the added volume of leads coming in. Clint and I both used the loan partner for help. That hire did not work out, but based on Jim's advice, we continued to look and hired again. That first semester I could really feel that my business was changing and my results were improving. All the extra work had begun to pay off.

In 2012, my business exploded. Josh was my coach in the first semester and really helped me make some technical changes to the way we were doing things. I learned to hire only experienced loan partners so that I could trust them and not have to check behind all their work. We hired Staci in February 2012, and she helped to propel our business. I had my best month ever three times in 2012. The market was great, and I ended up netting over $700,000 on my W2. WOW, what a difference after only 18 months in The CORE. I tripled my business and my income!

In 2013 we moved to a much larger office so that we would have the space to continue to grow our business. We grew the size of our team from just myself, Clint and Aly to a team of nine people in just 2.5 years! There were some growing pains, and not everyone we hired fit into our system, but with the guidance of The CORE we were able to make great strides in our team. 2013 saw some challenges in the market in the second half of the year, but I was still able to have a great year and had another W2 of $700,000.

2014 started off slow as well and we have had our challenges this year, but we are improving our business and always getting better at what we do. I will become a CORE coach in January 2015, and I am greatly looking forward to that opportunity.

I cannot say enough how appreciative I am for my CORE family. For Rick, Todd, and Reeta making this journey possible for me. I also want to thank all my coaches along the way: Jim Reed, Josh Sigman, Dave Kammerer, Hunter Marckwardt, Dixie Sanders, and Todd Scrima! The CORE has changed my life and given me the ability to do things I never thought would be possible. I remember thinking that if I joined this program, maybe I could make $500,000 "one day." The CORE has given me the ability to provide for my family and support my church and mission projects like I could not have dreamed. I am a firm believer that all good gifts come from God, and I believe that God led me to The CORE. My wife, Melissa, has been able to stop working and spend more time with our two awesome sons, Brayden and Jackson. Melissa has always supported me, and she is the reason behind my success in the mortgage business. Without her support I would not be able to do any of this.

Special thanks to Rick Ruby for believing in me – sometimes more than I believed in myself.

# Kendra Cooke

## Realtor Coach

## Location: Brentwood, Tennessee

## Started with The CORE: January 2006

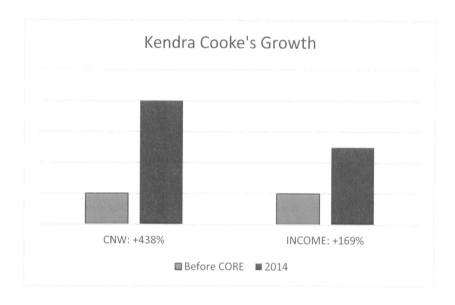

# Kendra Cooke

In October of 2005, I met a guy by the name of Brendan Donelson who was trying to earn my mortgage business. He showed up at a luncheon with a "Blue Beast." As our lunch started, numerous times I asked him what that book was. He nonchalantly said he was part of a coaching group, and if we had time later in the lunch hour, he would tell me about it. I continued to pressure him about it because honestly, I didn't care about desktop underwriting because I wasn't working on the file, and I personally couldn't change the rates he was quoting, so I was done with the "mortgage talk" and wanted to know more about "THAT BOOK." The tree on the back had gotten my attention, and I wanted to know more.

He proceeded to tell me he was part of a Real estate agent/lender coaching group out of Michigan, and it worked on your business, finances and life balance. I asked him, "How do I get in?"

His quick response was, "No one ever asks to get in. I have to sell them on it."

He let me know there was an event coming up in Palm Springs in just a couple weeks, and I signed up immediately and booked my trip. Not really knowing anything about the program, other than what he shared, but knowing I was broken, working too many hours, and had no money in the bank, I thought it was time to get some help.

Once at the Summit, I was fully engaged. I sat through classes learning tactics to implement right away to make some drastic changes in my business. Then after dinner each night, the owners and coaches continued to work with us around the fire or in the bar, so we felt like we got all we could from the event.

Each night I called my husband crying that I was so broken, so overwhelmed, and I so needed their systems, structure and accountability, but I didn't think we could afford it. With 100% support, he told me, "You can't afford to do it, and you cannot afford not to; either way you choose I support you."

So on Friday night as the Summit was wrapping up and Rick was requesting signed intent forms, I made a decision… not to sign my form. I thought I could go home and put things in place myself, get some money saved up, and come back in six months to sign up for coaching.

As I was leaving the building, I heard a voice coming from behind me that said, "Kendra, did you get your form signed?" I kept walking. Then I felt someone touch my shoulder, and I turned around to see Reeta Casey standing there. I told her my story: I couldn't afford to do it right now, but I couldn't afford not too, so I was heading home to do it on my own "for now." She suggested I come back in and speak to Rick because they thought I needed it now. I knew that too, but I was so scared to pull the trigger. After some tears and encouragement, I left my intent form signed in Palm Springs and headed home.

Two weeks later I had a call with Rick, and after some coaching, we started talking about my money. I will never forget the phrase Rick said to me that day, and it changed my life. He said, "You are one bad month away from bankruptcy."

You see, in my eyes, I was a rock star. I was having my best year ever, selling 204 houses for $32,000,000 (with an average sales price right at $100,000). I had a team, and I was the number one producer in my company for several years running. I had plaques galore, worked about 80 hours per week BUT what I didn't have was any money in the bank.

I told Rick after I left the Summit and came home to do my first profit and loss ever, I realized that I spent over $40,000 per month on my team and expenses before I made a dime, and that I only had $56,000 in the bank. That was my wake up call. I knew I had a lot of work to do, starting with cutting expenses. So the billboard and moving truck were gone, then the big team had to be cut, and as I dissected everything about the way I was doing business, I realized I had to surrender, and surrender quickly!

After graduating, I renewed for a second round of coaching, and during that time Rick asked me if I would like to be a coach. I felt like I was ready. Honestly coaching for me is a way I give back to my industry, but it also keeps me on my best game.

After nine years with The CORE, numerous great coaches and mentors, I am happy to say I just logged my best year ever, on so many levels. I broke $500,000 net taxable income, I work less than 40 hours per week, I have $1,000,000 total net worth and almost $800,000 in cash net worth. My marriage is amazing, I have an awesome relationship with my 16-year-old son, and our family is active in the community and church. My team consistently closes 175 transaction per year, I have an eight-person team that is very loyal and professional, and we have a very balanced business with re-sales, new construction, and buyer representation.

Thank you Rick, Reeta and Todd for the journey!

# Sasha Farmer

## Realtor

Location: Charlottesville, Virginia

Started with The CORE: July 2011

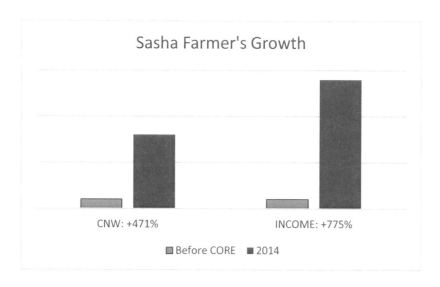

Sasha Farmer's Growth

CNW: +471%     INCOME: +775%

■ Before CORE   ■ 2014

# Sasha Farmer

I have been a student of The CORE for three years, a real estate agent for about seven years (starting in a down market), and I am 30 years old. In 2011 when I decided to join The CORE, my taxable income for the year was $70,000. I sold a fair amount of homes, but my expenses were high, and I was running my business haphazardly. By contrast, in 2014, my taxable income for June alone was $80,000, more than a year's worth of work just three short years ago. I am currently on track to make $400,000 in taxable income this year, as a 30-year-old, in a town that has one real estate agent for every 130 people. I never thought I'd say those words in all of my life, much less just a few years into my career. Without The CORE, I probably would have gone for years and years limiting my beliefs about what I could do because of what others in my market were doing.

After hours of advice and guidance from Kendra Cooke, Reeta Casey, Rick Ruby, and Dayton Schrader, I went from a single agent who thought I'd never have the consistency to hire even a part-time assistant or work fewer than 60 hours a week, to a five-person team, including myself, two full-time assistants, and two full-time buyers agents, working 45 hours a week with one Saturday or Sunday per month, maximum.

I have never been more motivated to do well in my business, not for the huge increases in income, but more for the time it affords me with my family, the security and peace of mind it allows, and the money it affords me to comfortably donate to my community. That is the whole mentality of The CORE: To run an extremely successful and profitable business so that you can make the lives of those you love and the community around you a better place.

Every time I waiver or struggle or have a tough day, I think of my long-time coach, Kendra Cooke, and try to think of what she would do, how she would handle it, or what she would say to me. The beauty of The CORE is that when I can't figure it out on my own, I just call or email Kendra, who is one of the most successful real estate agents in the country. She is a moment away and always willing to help.

I cannot say enough good things about this program. Yes, I am still one of the smaller fish in a sea of their incredibly successful real estate agents, but surrounding yourself with people bigger and more experienced is never a bad thing; it just opens your eyes to the endless opportunities and reminds you that limiting ideas and fears keep you from growing.

If you are willing to work hard, push outside your comfort zone, and accept change, then The CORE can have results above and beyond your highest expectations. Before you join, be sure to write down a goal for yourself that is completely unbelievable and seemingly unachievable so that you can experience the same sort of shock and surprise at your success just a few short semesters later.

# Jason Higham
## Lender Coach

## Location: The Woodlands, Texas
## Started with The CORE: January 2011

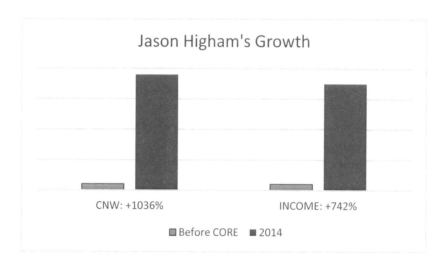

Jason Higham's Growth

CNW: +1036%          INCOME: +742%

Before CORE     2014

# Jason Higham

It was about 1990, I was 14 years old, and the hottest thing going for a 14-year-old kid was a Nintendo gaming system. All my friends had Nintendos. They got them for their birthday, or they got them for Christmas, so I thought the logical thing was to ask my dad for a Nintendo gaming system for my birthday.

My dad looked me in the eye and said, "Man, do you know how much those things cost?"

A Nintendo back in 1990 cost about 100 bucks, which for my father, who was a diesel mechanic and raising three boys on his single income, was just too much money to handle. It was too much money for a birthday present at that time. Whether he knows it or not, he taught me one of the most valuable lessons of my life.

He said, "We can't afford a Nintendo, but what you can do is go out with your lawn mower, and knock on doors, and ask people if you can mow their lawns. You can earn money while mowing grass, and you can buy a Nintendo yourself."

So that summer, I went knocking door to door with my dad's old lawn mower, asking people if I could mow their lawn for them. And keep in mind in Texas, in the subdivision where we lived outside of Houston, they were half-acre lots. And as I mowed those lawns that summer, I did all the work myself. I wrestled up some clients, and I would mow, edge, weed eat, and blow off the driveway for each half-acre lot at $10 a pop. I mowed grass all summer, I saved up my money, and I bought that dang Nintendo.

That was my first sales position, and I don't know if my dad knew this or not, but it was one of the most valuable lessons that I learned in my whole life. My dad taught me how to go get something I really wanted and to sell myself.

Working hard and doing all the work myself was actually ingrained in me from a very early age, so as I got into the mortgage business, I thought naturally I had to do all the work myself, but I didn't know how to delegate and build a team around me, not naturally at least. I got into the mortgage business when I was a junior in college. I was the first person to go to college in my family, and I went to Texas Christian University.

I looked at the girl next to me and said, "Hey I heard you're supposed to do an internship in college. What are you doing?"

She looked at me and said, "I'm working for this mortgage guy in Fort Worth, Texas. He used to play football, so he'll probably give you a job, too. You should call him up."

So, I called up Mike Harris and asked for an interview. I thought that since he played football too, I was a shoo-in for the job. I sat down with him, and he looked at me and said, "In 30 seconds or less I want you to tell me why you'd be a good hire and why you should come work for me." I sat there for about five seconds, thought about it, and told him I was a hard worker, that no one would outwork me. I told him I was a fast learner, competitive, and that most of all, I wanted an opportunity to learn, to be a sponge.

He looked me in the eye and he said, "The mortgage business is nothing more than selling yourself. If you can't sell yourself, you can't sell anybody else."

Those words have stuck with me and have been one of my most valuable lessons.

So I got in the mortgage business as an intern in college, and I've been doing it ever since. No one taught me how to go sell, and no one taught me how to go build a team, so from 2001 to 2008, I just worked really, really hard selling myself. That's all I did. I almost got out of the business during the downturn in 2008 just because no one had taught me the systems and structure of a business, how to talk to Real estate agents, or keep a database.

In 2009, my friend, Craig Ross, who was at the same mortgage company, invited me to the Summit in San Antonio. "You'd absolutely love it," he told me. I only went because it was close to my hometown, even though the cost of the Summit was more than my whole survival number. I took a leap of faith and went ahead. Coming from a sporting background and a military background (I also went to the United States Air Force Academy), I went to the Summit, and I sat by a campfire and listened to Rick Ruby.

My first impression of Rick and everyone sitting by the campfire was that I really didn't know if it was real or not. I just sat there in silence and just listened to the stories, and listened to this crazy guy talk about how to go get business, chase people down, and how to build relationships. I was very much engaged with the whole system and the whole CORE philosophy.

I left there and remember very specifically going to a dinner at the Summit and listening to a girl from California tell me how she had just done 16 loans in a month. I looked at her and, with all due respect, I thought to myself, "Wow, if she can do 16 loans in a month by doing these systems and building these teams, and taking good care of clients, all the things the CORE teaches, I can definitely do that."

I joined immediately. I didn't wait. I didn't mess around with it. I started the coaching, and I was impressed with Rick and the people that were in The CORE training and their quality of life and how they ran their businesses. I have to tell you that I really ate it up. I loved getting coached, and learning from others, and implementing, and so I took off pretty fast the first year. I almost doubled my production, and I definitely increased my savings.

In my second semester, my coach Todd Scrima taught me something that has stuck with me to this day. I was a young loan officer running a mortgage branch, and he was teaching me how to look at a P&L. I thought I had a pretty good month, but he told me that I needed to shut down my branch. I took that kind of personal, and I asked him why. He said, "Well, you don't have any other loan officers. It's just you, a processor, and a couple other support staff. By the time you net out the money, you'd be making the same amount as if you were just another loan officer somewhere. So either go find some loan officers, or shut down your branch."

That really motivated me. He made me get out of my comfort zone of calling up loan officers and recruiting them. That was a big "ah-ha" moment for me. I've been in The CORE for five years, and I've had plenty of ah-ha moments like that.

I've also grown personally. Before I joined The CORE, I was a single guy, flying by the seat of my pants. The CORE has not only changed me and taught me how to run a business, it's also taught me how to balance my life and become a better man in general. I do have them to thank for that. Since joining, I met my wife, got engaged at the Scottsdale training event, got married, and had two beautiful kids.

As I go through this journey in life and journey in business, I think the biggest thing The CORE has helped me with is keeping things in perspective, as well as being less emotional and more tactical about my business. I've learned how to build a team and a self-sustaining business so I can be home with my family. It's really drastically helped me settle down and become a good family man and a good person.

Since joining The CORE not only has my business increased, but my personal savings has increased ten times. That is something that is truly life changing for my family, especially growing up with a single income earner. I'm able to help change the legacy for my family and able to give back to the community tremendously.

When I started with The CORE, it was just me and a processor. Today I manage about 20 employees and four loan officers. We went from helping about 15 families a month and about 150 families a year, to this year when we'll help about 500 families.

The general outlook I have going into 2015 is one of optimism. I know that there is always going to be change, and it is how we deal with that change and who we surround ourselves with that really matter. One of the major reasons I joined is because I know that if you want to fly like an eagle, you have to hang out with eagles. I'm now a CORE coach, and I've learned way more teaching than I ever could have just being a student. It's really rewarding to help people find balance and purpose in both their businesses and personal lives, and watching the lightbulb go off.

My dream for the future is to continue to be a good family man, to help as many families as I can, and to help change the planet as much as humanly possible. My football coach, Gary Patterson, at Texas Christian University, always made practice much harder than the game. I learned so many valuable life lessons from him, including how to be a good man. Rick Ruby has definitely helped with how to deal with change and to keep things in perspective.

So, to close, I know I couldn't be where I'm at today without the lessons I learned from three important men in my life. I really want to thank my father, coach Gary Patterson at TCU, and finally, Rick Ruby and The CORE.

# PJ Johnson
## Lender

**Location:** San Diego, California

**Started with The CORE:** January 2015

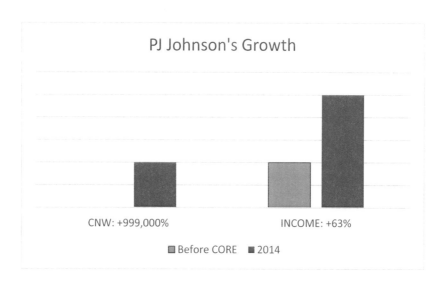

# PJ Johnson

I count my decision to attend my first Summit and eventually join The CORE as one of the three best decisions in my life besides coming to Jesus and marrying my wife Stephanie. It has revolutionized my life on every level.

I started in the business 17 years ago at the age of 20 with a box of cards and desk against the wall in the hallway.

"Good luck kid," they said.

And that was my training.

Fortunately I like to learn from others and had some excellent examples within my company. I would follow around the top producers, bring them coffee, food or their favorite beer in exchange for a few minutes to coach me. Within a year I was the top LO in the office and number five in the entire company, but I was doing it all wrong. I wish I had known of The CORE back then.

Fourteen years later I came to my first CORE Summit as the vice president of business development for a mortgage company. I had originated for 10 years but wanted to "move up" and look important. The reality was that I was miserable and stressed out and making less money than I did as an LO. I traveled two to three weeks a month, drank alcohol every day and was 30 pounds overweight. My friend Jeremy Forcier and I had been seminar junkies for years, and he said there was nothing like it and that I MUST go to this event. He told me it was a total game changer.

On the first day we connected with Greg Gale. I distinctly remember that I was inspired and filled with hope by the community of people and the possibilities for my future. I have so much respect for Greg and Jeremy, and they continue to encourage and push me to this day. Secretly I was contemplating going back to being a producing loan officer but was too fearful to leave my cushy salary and "title." On the last night of the Summit I encountered Rick Ruby, and in typical Rick fashion, he dissected me and had a plan in about 90 seconds.

I'll never forget his final words: "You need to stop wasting your time and get back to work as a loan officer, make some real money and spend more time at home and impacting the planet for Jesus."

I circled back with Forcier and Gale. I told them what Rick said, and they agreed and encouraged me to make it happen. It did not happen overnight for me. A year later my son Asher was born, and a month later, I spent 23 days on the road. I decided it was time to change.

In April 2012 I changed everything, resigned my job, and went to 100% commission. The craziest part was that I did not grow up in San Diego and had only been there a few years. Because I was traveling all the time, I had not developed a local network, so all my contacts and network were 10 hours north of me.

So, my referral network was starting at zero. I had not taken a loan application or looked at guidelines in five years, but with a 3-month-old and wife who wanted to stay home, the pressure was on. Some people might think I'm insane or super confident. The first may be true, but the second was not. I had so much anxiety and fear, but I trusted that God had put Rick and The CORE in my life for a reason, and I trusted The CORE does and will work if you are honest, willing, and open.

By the grace of God, I was also able to get sober and have remained so for three years in February 2015. Rick really encouraged me to stay strong and make the decision to do what was best for my family and myself. I'm so glad I had his support. I could not have done it without him in my life.

The results are jaw dropping to me at times. My first full year was more difficult than I had imagined on every level, and downright brutal at times, but having Rick motivating and pushing me developed in me a whole new level of resiliency and character that I needed to build the business. In 2013 I took home a net income of $251,000, lost 25 pounds, and paid down $60,000 in debt. The next year was more challenging for me than the first year with health issues, a new baby, and company problems getting me off to a very slow start. However I finished 2014 with a net income of $265,000. We finished the last three months on a run making between $39,000 and $47,000 per month and paying down my debts from $250,000 to $60,000.

I love Rick Ruby and The CORE. I have 25 close friends in The CORE now, and they have all tripled or quadrupled their business. It's simply incredible to watch the growth. This year I'm on track to make over $500,000 and will continue to grow my team and branch into the top producing office in California.

# Haley Garcia

## Realtor Coach

**Location:** The Woodlands, Texas

**Started with The CORE:** January 2012

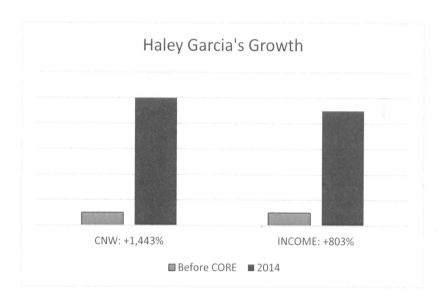

Haley Garcia's Growth

CNW: +1,443%        INCOME: +803%

■ Before CORE  ■ 2014

# Haley Garcia

Just three short years ago I was asked to attend a Summit event by a very good lender friend of mine. He had asked me to come with a group of Real estate agents many times before, but I had always been too busy to even stop and think about what the event might offer.

At the point when I received the invitation I had just left the ER from what I thought was a brain aneurism. Luckily it ended up being just being a panic attack; however, it came on due to the stress and work load. I actually looked at attending this event as a vacation and figured, "What do I have to lose?" At this point in my life I had been divorced, was working approximately 80 hours each week, if not more during most weeks, and was barely keeping my head above water. I had been a $10 to $15 million producer for 10 years, so I made a decent living and thought I had a good book of business, but I knew it was wearing me out at a very young age.

What I hadn't slowed down to realize was at this point I had no life, no relationships with meaning, and basically ran around, always trying to please my clients so they would be happy and keep sending me business; never once did I stop to think about what might make me happy. By this point I was just always wanting more. Looking back now, I see how greedy that was. I had even decided to open my own Brokerage, thinking that I could somehow create a secondary revenue, while still selling and doing what I love, but also by broadening my income streams. I quickly learned that being a producing owner/broker was no way to live, nor was the income from the Brokerage remotely worth the blood, sweat, and tears it took to run the shop.

It was about this time that I met Rick Ruby at my first Summit. I will never forget what he said to me:

"So let me get this straight, movie star. You fell down, you hit your head and you decided to open a company?"

Well the answer to that was yes. And now I was an agent without any systems or structure, I had no ideas where my leads came from, not a clue how much revenue I generated each deal, and honestly couldn't tell you how much I truly made each year. I was also a run-down owner/broker who looked exhausted, felt exhausted, and was now investing every dollar I earned into a firm that was only paying me back a profit of $20,000 per year! All the while my personal business was dying due to me devoting so much time and energy into the firm that truly wasn't even paying me.

I remember Rick telling me to think about whether the $20,000 per year could be made up by selling ONE more house per year. I thought, "Well isn't that a genius idea!" With all that I learned at the Summit and with the advice of Rick, I was determined I was going to join this group called The CORE. But more than that, I made a choice and promised myself I was going to do exactly what they told me to. This wasn't going to be easy for me; I'm headstrong, don't like to be told what to do, and I consider myself to be an intelligent person. However, it doesn't take long for me to see through to the bottom of things, and I could clearly see that everyone involved with The CORE was genuine. Each person I encountered had been through hard times, had learned how to weather the storm, how to make better decisions both personally and in business, and now had made such great progress that these coaches were willing to teach us all they had learned along their journey.

Throughout my two years as a student The CORE coaches helped me negotiate the sale of my firm, restructure my business, and really learn to focus on the streams of business that I generate leads from. They also helped me realize that my database and my relationships are the most important aspect of real estate – Not the glossy magazine ads that I'd spent thousands of dollars on only to be another real estate agent in another magazine. I learned how to build and grow my team, how to truly be a leader, and how to be a grateful, gracious, generous person. Even though I felt I was all of those things prior to The CORE, I wasn't living my life in a way that showed them.

Joining The CORE was truly the best decision I have ever made, as cliché as that sounds. It has changed my life in so many ways. I immediately signed up at the end of that first Summit, and I remember thinking, "I hope they take me." I was such a mess at the time, I knew it was a possibility that they would not. But if that happened I was determined to just keep applying until they did. I was mortified about them reviewing my tax returns, for them to know how little cash I had and the amount of debt I had accrued. But I also knew I had to start somewhere, and putting my head in the sand would do nothing but make things worse and prolonged.

So after the painful part of realizing I had worked for 10 years and had only saved $10,000, still had $5,000 in debt, and still owed the IRS for that years' taxes still, I decided to go to work and get myself straight! I did exactly what I was told, just as I had promised myself I would do. Some days were extremely difficult. Some days

I wanted to give up. But quitting was not an option; I am not a quitter. I simply pushed through, even on the days there were tears streaming down my face, nothing stopped me!

I went from netting $225,000 in the year that I became a coaching student to last year, the year I graduated, when I netted $615,000. It still feels surreal. I can't believe that I am the same girl who used to show 40 houses in a weekend and had not taken a weekend off for 10 years. Now I rarely work weekends, don't work more than 40 hours a week, have hobbies, relationships I love to be part of, friends I spend time with and an amazing team to help me run my business!

Upon graduation I was asked if I wanted to be a coach. My first thought was, "Of course I do, but I don't want to let anyone down." Then I realized if I could help one person realize their potential, one person straighten out their priorities or one person learn how to manage their business so that they could enjoy their family and their life, then coaching was exactly where I needed to be. That is what all of the great coaches gave to me, and I am honored to have the opportunity to give it back.

This short trip of being part of The CORE family is a lifetime journey, but it has taken me so little time to realize all the potential that life has to offer. Never stop learning and growing.

# Dave Kammerer

## Lender Coach

**Location:** Eugene, Oregon

**Started with The CORE:** January 2004

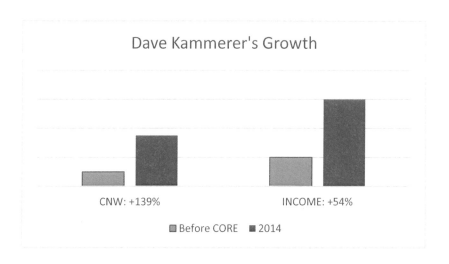

# Dave Kammerer

It was November 2003, and I was heading to my first CORE Training Summit in San Antonio. I was just coming off a tremendous year of business. I had just finished my second year in a row at number one in production for my company in the Northwest region, my best year ever so far.

I was not happy though.

Why not? The past year had seen me at work more than 80 hours per week on average, and I would often go days at a time without seeing my kids. My marriage was at a low point, mainly because we were not spending any time together, and when we did get some time, I would be on the phone with a client. Clearly I was not on top of my life. In addition, the interest rates were on the rise, and I still had fear EVERY month that no loans would close and this would be the end of my business. I would not get paid and my family would suffer. I knew I needed help, and the company I worked for did not have any examples of how to do this right.

A loan officer competitor invited me to see this guy Rick Ruby in San Antonio, Texas. I would later see this as a selfless gift. I say "selfless" because she knew that inviting me would help me become a stronger force in our business and create more competition. I have never forgotten that and follow that same path of sharing the greatness that is potentially in all of us. Note to self: Watch the movie "Pay it Forward" again.

As for San Antonio. The catch was I had to take three days off and pay for the trip and a seminar. It was going to cost me $3,500 or more total. I had never paid anywhere near this much to advance my business. It was time. I knew I needed help and had been praying for some guidance. This was my answer, so I went on faith to San Antonio. In many ways I felt this was my last chance to save my personal life and keep my business life intact somehow.

This was my first CORE Training Summit. I sat at the table doing the Wheel of Life for the first time with tears as I described to my table mates how my love life was a three and maybe even worse. My money looked good, or so I thought, at $360,000 cash net worth. I knew right then that money was only a measurement of my ability to live within my means, and that so many other things in my life were a mess. I had low family, love life, spiritual, work and self ratings. I was two for seven. My wheel was bent badly and I finally knew what I needed to do: Get a coach and work on all of it a bit at a time.

Rick and Todd were on stage that Thursday and Friday inspiring and coaching, and above all, I knew they were telling me the truth. They were not perfect either, but I wanted what they had and what they were striving for. I saw the other coaches and spoke to all of them during the breaks and meals. None of them were selling me, but rather, sharing their experience and then asking me all about me. It was encouraging. I felt a breakthrough coming. I had hope answered and renewed again. Little did I know this was just the beginning of a great journey.

All of us have some experience or several experiences that contribute to who we are. I look back and see the young man, father and husband of my youth going through a home-buying experience. Twenty-two years ago, before I was a professional loan rep, I was a borrower who needed a loan like many I have met since. What was it like?

My wife and I were really excited and nervous at the same time. We'd just had our third child and we were outnumbered, so the world has really changed for us. We were dirt poor and living paycheck to paycheck. On top of that, we were in the process of buying and selling our home. We'd just sold our first home and netted $14,000. This was the most money I had ever had at one time. I was thinking that this homeownership thing was a pretty good deal.

We were moving up to a better home in a better neighborhood, and that was a big part of our current anxiety. We really needed this for our family. We had the means and were looking forward to this move because our home had sold, and we were getting out of what we knew was a rough neighborhood for our kids. They would grow up in a safer environment and have some stable friends nearby. I'd never really thought about how important this was until we had our own family and now I understood why both our parents worked so hard to make sure we had a good home in a good neighborhood.

There was one major hurdle, and that was our mortgage lender. They were taking way longer than we'd expected based on our first experience and also what our Real estate agent, Mike, had told us to expect. We were more than 60 days past our original closing date. We wanted to be moved before the baby came and that did not happen. So with our lives full of that extra chaos, the stress of not knowing for sure when we could move was taking its toll. We were living in a duplex rental month to month and for sure did not want to be there very long.

Mike then came up with a great solution, or so we thought. He convinced the seller to let us move in prior to closing on the assurance from the lender we would get closed eventually. We thought this was great and trusted in the process. What happened next forever changed the way I look at business, and in particular, what is now my industry and profession.

We moved in. The loan still did not close. The lender did not perform, and we were in a rate market that had increased substantially when our lock term ran out. We no longer qualified. Being a young man and not knowing much of our industry, I tried in vain to come up with a solution. I learned much about the loan business during this time. I learned that it was very likely the lender I was using did not manage my file properly. The only reason given for the delay was that it was taking extra time to underwrite due to mortgage insurance. Nine weeks in MI underwriting was a bit out of the ordinary, I discovered later.

In the end it did not matter because the train had left the station, so to speak. I felt completely abandoned by our lender, and we had to move back out of this home. It was mortifying for us. My Real estate agent was quick to help with a solution. We ended up in a home half the size with private financing and stuffed our three kids into one bedroom, instead of three bedrooms, for the next two years. Within a month I lost my father suddenly to an aggressive form of cancer. Shortly afterwards I decided to change careers and industries. These two experiences were the catalyst for major change in my life.

I learned much from this experience about business, business people, my family and my lovely wife. Sherrie is truly a blessing, and she is full of grace and faith. We made it work and stuck together. She gave me strength often, and I gave it back to her. Every experience, good or bad, is a blessing to be thankful for.

Here is the big one: I am not in control of most things.

At that point in my life, I still did not get that, and I allowed that fact to frustrate me. The good part was I turned that energy into action every single day to affect positive change in my family and my life.

The mortgage business really caught my attention, and through this experience, I learned a tremendous amount about how things work. Of course I was interested based on personal experience, and I really needed to know why it went so wrong compared to my first home loan. After seeking counsel with trusted business folks, I decided to become a loan officer because I knew I could do it better than what we had just experienced.

I interviewed, began my career, and never looked back. It was a natural fit. I promised myself never to let anyone down the way it had happened to my family, and I would always be sure to find a solution for the people that depended on me, both Real estate agents and buyers. This was a big deal.

Back to San Antonio. I signed up for coaching and committed to the two years. I was placed in a group with some peers and a coach from the other side of the country.

Brothers and Sisters, did I struggle!

I was bad at the homework, except for the Pay Log and Personal Budget. Interesting. I look back now, and it makes complete sense. I did the things best that I was already good at. I had to get better. It was not until my third semester that I truly surrendered. Now I know how important that word is in action. It simply means to do what I am told and not to question it.

Go on faith: A great lesson that has since served me well and may be the most important lesson of all. Have faith and trust your leader to guide you. Wisdom will provide for a complete and an everlasting life.

I began to coach the business partners around me. I was a natural, and it helped me be accountable to myself too. Another interesting discovery. After two years, I was a graduate and I was invited to remain in coaching. There was no question I still needed it, and I had not won a dragon yet. I wanted one badly, mostly because it would mean that I was the best student of a coaches group, and I am very competitive. Also as I discovered that my love language is "words of praise." I liked it when someone told me I was doing well, and I really liked to please everyone.

At that time it dawned on me that I might one day become a coach with The CORE Training. What an honor. I knew I wanted to be associated and in relationship with Rick, Todd, Reeta and all the other coaches. They were not only my mentors, but had also become friends and people I truly cared about.

Something else was happening to me. I no longer had any fear about my business continuing. Confidence was real in my life and my business now. Before I would often say to myself, "Fake it until you make it." Being authentic had become more important, and I was no longer afraid to tell anyone my truth.

As I grew in business and life, The CORE Training became a part of me, just like I had become part of The CORE Training. I looked up to and admired the group of coaches and wanted more of that in my life. I told Rick Ruby and Todd Scrima that I had the stuff to be a coach, and I needed to know that they wanted of me to join their team. Rick was direct and honest as usual.

The good: I was a great husband and father, and my business was consistent. I had money in the bank. Rick liked that example.

The bad: I was soft, both physically and in my business life.

Rick told me the truth: I was overweight, out of shape, and I had developed some poor habits around my health. Strong people take criticism and use it to improve. Weak people let it crush them. Rick was right. I was determined to make some changes. With Sherrie's help I started to change my habits around food and exercise. What I found is that there are three things important to my health:

1. Eating good food in smaller amounts more often – this one is tough when you don't follow systems very well.

2. Getting at least seven hours of sleep every night. This one surprised me, but it is true. My body needs to rest to become better.

3. Getting exercise every single day, four days a week of intensity and the other three at least 30 minutes of something that moves your blood like walking fast or hiking or biking.

It took me six months, and I dropped 35 pounds and improved my health so much that my doctor took me off a blood pressure medication I had been on for at least four years. To this day I still struggle with staying consistent, and like many things in business, I have developed habits and a system to help me. I really admire Rick on this one because he has led with an example of staying in great condition these last couple of years. I will catch up to him. It took me 20 years to get out of shape, so it will take some significant time to get where I want to be. I am on my way, and this had added not only years to my life, but a higher quality as well.

So, Rick, Reeta, and Todd took me in as a coach. I found out later that the other coaches had voted me in. What an honor to be chosen by such a fantastic peer group! Thank you to all of those coaches because this has changed my life permanently for the better.

# Brian Kludt

## Lender Coach

**Location**: Germantown, Wisconsin

**Started with The CORE**: January 2012

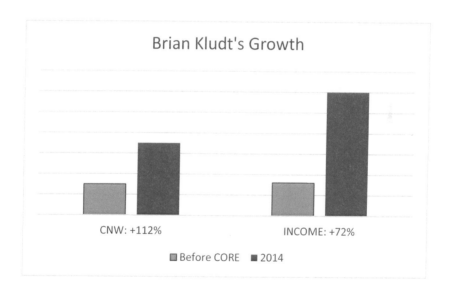

Brian Kludt's Growth

CNW: +112%          INCOME: +72%

■ Before CORE  ■ 2014

# Brian Kludt

My CORE journey began in September 2011. I was invited to speak at a Todd Duncan event about how to build a successful Real estate agent-based business model. The irony of the event never ceases to amaze me. In 2010 I had generated a total of 42 leads from the real estate industry, and yet I was on stage speaking to mortgage originators across the country on how to be successful with real estate agents. To say I lacked credibility was an understatement.

Moments after my presentation, Jeremy Forcier spoke to the group about how to structure a successful sales week. Unlike the other presenters who shared complicated-yet-flashy business-generating ideas, Jeremy walked around with a one-page document in his hand and proceeded to walk through a simple yet tactical strategy on how he was able to prospect 20-plus hours per week. I was introduced to the infamous Greatness Tracker!

Having known Jeremy through the "speaking circuit" gig, I accosted him offstage as I had to ask more questions about his new model. He told me that he had met Rick Ruby and The CORE and that it had changed his life. Having come off a rather successful year of making $500,000, deep down I knew my house of cards was built on a series of refi waves. Unless I did something dramatic, I was in deep trouble when the inevitable interest rate increase hit the market. I would not be a casualty. I needed a major transition.

Thirty days later, I attended my first Summit in San Diego. I was struck by the lack of flash, stage shows, or "celebrity" names within the mortgage industry. I was skeptical. I literally almost flew home after the first day because I heard very little that I had never heard before. In my hotel room that night, however, a burning question hit me: *"If you've heard all of these things before, why aren't you doing them?"*

On the second day of the Summit I sat with Dave Kammerer, who helped me see a vision of what my world and life could look like in ten years. I was hooked. I completed my intent form and was ready for my coaching interview. Or so I thought. I interviewed with Rick, and within minutes he told me he thought he'd have trouble with me. He said I was "too big" and that my ego would get in the way. Only if I agreed to completely surrender would he take me on. I assured him I needed to change or die and that I would be a good soldier. I was accepted into coaching to start in January 2012!

I started coaching with Jimmy Reed and struggled mightily my first semester. I was convinced that I could "pick and choose" the elements of The CORE that would work for me and disregard the rest. I made headway with some new relationships with Real estate agents, but I still struggled to put the pieces together.

Three months into coaching, I called Jimmy and told him I didn't think The CORE was a fit. The pressure was getting to me, and I asked him to back off. At the May Summit Rick and Jimmy taught a class on leadership. In the middle of class, Rick started talking about how frustrated he was with one of his students because he wasn't "playing all out." He then went on to explain how this student called his coach to complain about how hard his coach was on him… and I realized he was talking about me.

It was my moment of decision: Would I crack under the pressure, or would I step up and step into the heat once and for all. I jumped up to the stage and told Rick to BRING IT ON. From that point forward I've understood deeper levels of change and surrendered to the realization that the ONLY way to change is to humble yourself, to trust, and to surrender.

In 2013 I generated over 450 Real estate agent leads, ten times as many in 2011, the year before I began my CORE journey. My team and branch have exploded. I started with one and half team members and now have five. I now run the entire greater Milwaukee area branches of Waterstone Mortgage with 18 loan officers. My production is virtually 100% purchase-based. I built my dream lake home, paid off over $60,000 in consumer debt, and tripled my cash net worth. In March 2014 I was able to leave for the first true one-week vacation of my mortgage career: NEVER checking email, NO calls on my cell phone from clients, real estate agents, or my team!

I graduated my two-year journey with The CORE in November 2013 and was invited to become a coach. I am so honored to be working with the BEST of the best and helping other CORE students reach their potential, overcome self-limiting beliefs, and changing the planet. I continue to be humbled daily and recognize that the path to growth is endless, the pursuit of excellence is never-ending, and that serving others is my purpose.

Thank you Rick, Todd, Jim, and Josh, my first four coaches for changing my life. I am forever committed to growth, to change, and "paying it forward."

# Amber Griffin

## Realtor


**Location**: Houston, Texas

**Started with The CORE**: January 2013

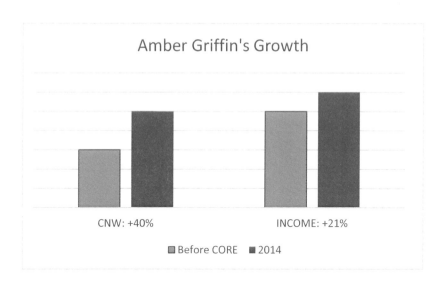

# Amber Griffin

Dear Rick Ruby,

Where do I begin to express the profound ways this program and its coaches have CHANGED my life? I honestly don't know because The CORE has impacted every aspect of my existence.

The very first Summit I attended was in Indian Wells, California, in November 2012. I had heard about The CORE from your coach and student Jennifer Hernandez. I was already enrolled in your CD program when I arrived at the Summit. Even then it was only at Jennifer's insistence that I go. You see, I really didn't think I could afford to spend the entry fee, flight, and hotel to attend. Jennifer said, "You can't afford not to. Just get here and you can room with me." I was completely blown away by the classes, coaches, and students from around the country. By the end of that Summit, I had signed a letter of intent to be coached as a real estate agent. Being a woman of God, I took a HUGE leap of faith, believing that God would provide. Thankfully He has provided in abundance, and that is just the beginning.

In December 2012, I officially began my journey as a coaching student with The CORE. Prior to this, I was a team of one and had never kept a budget, a monthly accounting of my business, or personal finances. I was buried in relocation business and had almost zero hours to prospect or network. I had a dismal existence and very little fun. I was exhausted all the time. My "Wheel of Life" was completely out of balance, but I was in denial about it. In January 2013 I hired a part-time RP1 who became full time within a few months, and in July I made my second hire, a dialer/business development assistant.

The CORE helped me take a closer look at my life, and I did not like what I saw. It was very painful to peel back the layers of my life that I had covered up or was in denial about. After close examination, I realized I needed to make changes that were big, changes that were painful. I had to be broken down in order to rebuild. The CORE has and continues to teach me how to be a leader and a giver, sharing more with others.

With the help of God and The CORE, my net profit after one year was 37 percent greater. I have doubled my savings, and I have only touched the tip of the iceberg. I was also able to join the Houston West Chamber where I currently serve as an ambassador, I was accepted into the West Houston Leadership Institute, and I am now networking and building relationships with business people.

The CORE encouraged me to attend "Rapport Leadership - Break Through," and I cannot begin to share how much more confidence I now have in every aspect of my life. The CORE helped me to believe in myself and inspired me to achieve more. I now know that anything that I set my mind to and work hard at is possible. Before The CORE, I did not believe that. I lived in the small box of my comfort zone, but now I am stretching way beyond that box to places I never even dreamt of. I am setting goals and reaching them and have huge personal ambitions I am working toward as well. I also have a hobby too: I am learning to play golf.

Last but not least, I met a gentleman by the name of Rick Johnson at the one-day Mega event in Dallas in

February 2014. Rick is a real estate agent from Oregon whom Dave Kammerer invited to attend. Jennifer Hernandez (again) invited me to ride up with her to Dallas from Houston to get a refresher between Summits. Rick and I met Friday evening after the day's event and talked at length. We exchanged information and have been in constant contact ever since. I have visited Oregon and he has visited me in Houston. We have July 4th plans back in Oregon for a (very) long weekend and again in the Texas Hill Country in August.

Thank you CORE, Jennifer, Dave (and God) for bringing the two of us together! We couldn't be happier and both believe this is the beginning of a new fantastic journey. I am so grateful for you, the entire CORE, and all the coaches that inspire me!

Sincerely,
Your future coach

# Mark Kuchik

## Lender Coach

## Location: Carmel, Indiana
## Started with The CORE: January 2006

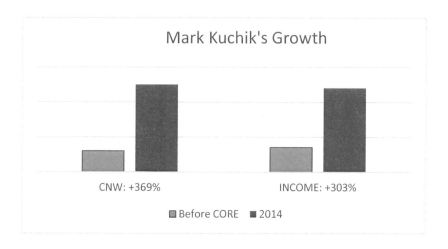

# Mark Kuchik

My CORE journey started in early 2005. At that time, my business was just me as the loan originator and my wife, Rhonda who did *some* processing and mainly cultivated real estate agent relationships for me. I was in my third year as a member of By Referral Only. I learned a great deal with this organization, and my business was starting to take off. Now I had a new challenge: How would I handle all of this business? At this point, it was obvious I needed help with growing my team and operation. Another BRO student, Jeanette Hartman, suggested we look at The CORE Training to help with advanced needs in operations.

In May 2005, Rhonda attended the Summit in New York. I couldn't (actually chose not to) go for two reasons: 1) I wasn't running a true business. I was a one-man shop and wasn't able to take three days out of the office. 2) I wasn't willing to spend another $1,750 for a second attendee to The Summit. Looking back, WOW was I a mess! I agreed to let Rhonda go even though the $1,750 tuition plus airfare and hotel was about ten times more than I was comfortable with. In addition, I knew they *had* to be selling you something, right? So before she left, I looked at The CORE website, and of course I saw they want you to join their program for $2,000 a month, and it was a 2-year commitment. My reaction? There is nobody who is going to be able to deliver enough value

162

to justify spending $48,000. I prepared Rhonda that she was NOT to commit to anything while she was at the event.

At the New York Summit, Rhonda was so excited about the content she learned in just the first session that she couldn't resist calling me to tell me some of the tactics she learned in that first hour or so. She went on and on about this guy, Rick Ruby. Let me tell you, if you aren't there to see it for yourself, there isn't anyone in this world who can describe Rick Ruby. Those who have met this man will understand. More on what Rick did to change my life later!

After Rhonda returned from the Summit, we actually implemented a few things and sure enough, we saw results – this thing was working! Next it was time to sign up for the November Summit, and Rhonda was pushing me hard to go with her this time. Again, I could not justify the expense but did agree to go (honestly only to make my wife happy).

The first night at the event, I got to speak to Rick, and within the short walk from dinner to the fire pit outside the hotel, Rick gave me <u>Lesson #1</u>: That I brought more value to my clients than I thought at that time. I was essentially "giving it away" to my clients. Rick gave me three specific changes to make in my business when I returned. I did not know it at the time, but these three changes paid for my two-year ($48,000) commitment within the first six months of being a coaching student. Understanding my self-worth was my first life-changing lesson from The CORE!

Later that night at the fire pit, I listened to and overheard other students talk about their revenue and savings numbers. At the time, I thought I was doing pretty well but I was hearing people who were saving $400,000 per year, with incomes of $600,000 per year.

These numbers were nowhere close to being feasible to me. I vividly remember standing there an hour into the whole event and saying to myself, "I would be a fool not to join The CORE."

If you have been to the November Summits, you know that the theme is goal setting. One exercise Todd Scrima had the room do was to close our eyes and DREAM as BIG as we could. What did our lives look like in five years? How much money would we be making? How much would we have saved? How many people on our teams? How many loans would we be closing? I will never forget looking over at what Rhonda put down for her answers, and I literally laughed out loud. I said to her, "Honey, he said dream, but you still have to be realistic." I immediately looked at my answers and soon realized that I was thinking way to small. I bumped my answers up a little, but was nowhere near the level Rhonda was thinking. Guess what? Rhonda hit her five-year dream goal in 4.5 years!

Lesson #2: Dream bigger than ever and know that anything is possible. There are dozens of living examples of fairy tale stories inside The CORE.

I am proud to say that I did graduate from the two-year program. I might add that Rick called me a "slow student" as I approached to receive my award on stage. He went as far to ask me in front of 300 people why I was a slow student. At the time, many people came up to me because they felt bad for me that Rick had called me out on stage. Honestly, it did not bother me one bit because he was right! I was a slow student. It wasn't because I didn't work hard, it was because I did not SURRENDER.

Surrendering is getting out of your own way and just doing what The CORE tells you to do. I always had a reason why I should put my own spin on things.

Lesson # 3: Just do what you are told and trust your mentors and the system. You will always get where they want you to be in results. However, it's up to you to determine how quickly you get there.

Growing your business and team comes with growing pains. Just when you think you have it figured out, something changes. In 2009, our branch was growing as we were hiring more loan officers, LPs and processors. There seemed to be something not clicking. There seemed to be something off. We were working hard, but my production numbers seemed to hit a ceiling, and from a management standpoint, it sure seemed to be harder than it should be as Rhonda and I co-managed the branch. Can you believe Rick decided to do a site visit and get us back on track? I am completely wowed that he would take the time to do an actual visit, but he did and still does to this day for students.

At his visit, Rick did his thing and asked a lot of questions. He summed up our problem and fixed it within a three-minute speech. Simply put, he said, Mark, you originate loans. Rhonda, you run the branch. Mark, you don't run the branch anymore, and Rhonda you do not originate mortgages, got it? Simple answers to what seemed to be a complex problem at the time.

Lesson #4: Keep it simple. Do not over complicate the matter at hand. To this day, Rick has the most simplistic answers, and he is right every single time!

Lesson #5: Delineate clear job responsibilities.

As hard as the mortgage industry got from 2008 to 2012, I am proud to say that our business took off and we were having record years. We had a CORE system and we followed it. While most loan originators were confused and scared during the unprecedented mortgage meltdown, I had my army CORE of mentors behind me. When I needed to go from broker to banker, I had my army to guide me through any important decisions. Any challenge you can think of having, I had my army to guide me. We took over the local market share and my income went from $350,000 in 2010 to $550,000 in 2011 to $1 million in 2012. Things couldn't have been any better. While my friends in the business were struggling and some getting out of the business, The CORE ensured that I succeeded, and I did.

Once you think you have it all figured out, things change quickly. For me this was 2011. I had just come off a record year, but I couldn't do it anymore. I needed to take some time to recharge. At the time, I didn't know it, but I had hit an emotional bottom. I realized that I had not taken any true vacations and needed to truly unplug. More importantly, I realized that I was not having fun because I didn't have the right team setup. I didn't have "A" players, and I was a poor leader. I didn't understand at the time that there is a huge difference between being a manager and a leader. There were a few lessons that came out of this timeline:

Lesson #6:  Always be recruiting. Recruit every day of your life, even if you don't need someone today. This creates a "virtual bench" of future employees. For some reason, when you don't need to hire, the "A" Players show up. Prior to this, I would hire people out of desperation. I always knew there were flaws in who I was hiring, but I would justify why it would be okay. This lesson was a true game changer for me!

Lesson #7: Many of us sales people tend to be very emotional people. When problems or challenges arise, it's hard to get past the emotions. That is why many sales people in our business struggle. I learned from Todd Scrima the importance of learning to be "tactical" versus "emotional." When challenges arise, you can learn from the experience, but you can never change what happened in the past. So a tactical person moves on and forward and doesn't dwell. The more tactical and less emotional you become, the more successful you will be. Todd Scrima – thank you for this one! Another game changer.

Lesson #8:  I am learning daily that being a great leader is where you see big jumps in income. I always thought being a manager and leader were the same thing. Being a great leader is where the magic happens. Getting your team to believe in you, empowering them and having them willing to do anything for you is a result of being a true leader. At this moment in time, I would say that I am about 20% a great leader. This is a learned skill and one that I don't think you ever stop learning. The leadership skills that I get by listening to Todd and Rick are invaluable. Learning to be a better leader has made this journey so much more fun. I have found that more people follow you and respect you the more leadership skills you possess.

The CORE has always been about changing the planet. The focus of helping others who don't have what you have became a big focal point in 2012. I have to be honest, up that point in my life, I gave to charities here and there, but for the most part, I was selfish and felt like I worked hard for my money and really only helped on a small scale. Over the past couple of years, I have realized how fortunate I am to be in a position to help others. Spiritually, I am a better person knowing what an impact I have made to others by giving to those in need and supporting charities I believe in. I am especially proud to say that The CORE organization donated $3.5 million to others in 2013.

The CORE is nothing sexy. In fact, it's about simple, super basic activities and tactics. Quite frankly we are learning the same basic tactics from the day I started in 2005. It is truly amazing how the Partners in The CORE as well as the coaches have reinvented themselves year after year and Summit after Summit. In my eight-year run with The CORE, I have attended all but one Summit. I can honestly say that I am truly blown away with what The CORE presents to its students each time. There is a reason I continued to pay $2,000 per month beyond the initial two-year commitment. At one point, I tallied up that I paid over $170,000 in tuition to the CORE. To many that number is insane, but the return on investment has been priceless. I went from a closed-minded loan originator with $80,000 in the bank to a loan officer averaging 23 loan closings a month with more than $650,000 in the bank. The system works, period!

I am now on the inside of The CORE since becoming a coach in January 2013. When I sit in a room with Rick, Todd, Reeta and the rest of The CORE coaches and staff, I can't help but think what it must have been like in 1975 when Bill Gates was sitting in a room talking to his people about a new company called Microsoft that was going to change the planet. I truly feel The CORE is changing the planet, and I am forever grateful for what The CORE family has done for me and my family. I am truly blessed to have each and every one of you in my life! Most importantly, I have to thank my wife Rhonda. Without you having the vision and pushing me to attend The CORE Summit in 2005, we wouldn't have reached the levels we have.

# Allison Lord

## Lender

## Location: Kirkland, Washington

## Started with The CORE: January 2014

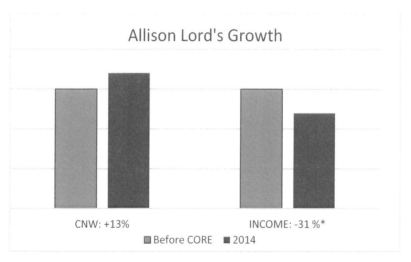

*Allison Lord's Growth*

CNW: +13%          INCOME: -31 %*

■ Before CORE   ■ 2014

*\* Allison's numbers reflect a transition from an inflated focus on refinance business to a consistent focus on purchase business.*

# Allison Lord

It was the summer of 1999, and I was a high school graduate getting ready to start college in the fall. My five-year vision was set: I would have my bachelor's degree in elementary education, my teaching certificate, be married with two kids, a dog, a white picket fence and working as an elementary educator.

Boy was I wrong!

That summer I was hired as an administrative assistant at First Horizon Home Loans. It was just supposed to be a summer job. Instead, it turned into a college job that turned into my life's passion.

In December of 2001, I was offered a job at a small start-up mortgage company named Cobalt Mortgage. There were only five of us on my first day – the president, the vice president, the processing manager, my mother-in-law Carol, who was our operations manager, and myself. For the first three months, the phone barely rang. By Spring 2002, we had about 50 employees, and I began really learning the ins and outs of the lending world. As the company grew, I was promoted first to processing assistant, then loan officer assistant and then to junior loan officer. In January of 2006, we had more than 500 employees and I decided it was time to go out on my own and become a loan officer.

I will always remember my first meeting as a loan officer with Ernie, the owner of Cobalt. I sat in his office and he asked me, "What's your business plan? Who's in your sphere? What agents are you going to target?" I sat for a moment and realized I had no clue what I was doing. The past seven years of training may have taught me how to structure and close a loan, but I was in the dark on how to get business, gain relationships, and keep them! For the next six years I floundered. I made decent income, more than I ever would as a teacher, but always knew there had to be more.

I will never forget the day that I was introduced to The CORE. Cobalt hired a new loan officer that was placed in the office next to me. She was beautiful, stylish, full of energy, and closed a TON of business. I on the other hand was averaging $1.2 million per month and barely making $100,000 a year. I observed Jolene running from appointment to appointment, having a full schedule, and closing loans gracefully. I on the other hand was pregnant and finding myself beginning to slip out of focus. One day I stopped her and asked her "How are you doing it?" My business changed in an instant! Jolene showed me the Greatness Tracker. My business doubled that year, and I even had a baby. For the first time I made more than $200,000. I continued to fill out the Greatness Tracker for the next year. I again increased my income to $250,000 while pregnant with my second child.

In January 2014 I began my coaching journey. I was nine months pregnant, about to go on maternity leave, but if The CORE was going to take me, I was going to do it. As Rick Ruby told me, in my first semester I was a terrible student. I did not fill out the forms, barely closed loans, and lost 30 percent of my referral partners while I was on maternity leave. I was a mess! However, The CORE is what pulled me out.

My second semester with Jen Hernandez was a game changer. I began working full time again. My forms were complete and correct, and I began making my calls, holding events, and WOW my business turned around. Although my 2014 was lower than my previous two in income and loan volume, I know that without The CORE, I would not have been able to turn things around as fast as I did.

I have learned that there is no "easy" button. Instead, I know that through hard work, consistency, and surrendering, great things will come.

# Allen Huggins

## Realtor Coach

**Location:** Nashville, Tennessee

**Started with The CORE:** July 2008

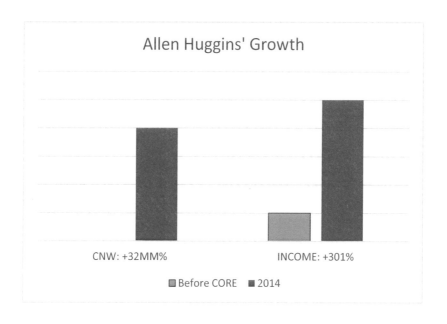

Allen Huggins' Growth

CNW: +32MM%  INCOME: +301%

■ Before CORE  ■ 2014

# Allen Huggins

Thanks to The CORE, I am no longer a real estate agent, but a business owner.

My story begins in my hometown of Nashville, TN. I grew up in a family of real estate agents and mortgage bankers, so it was natural when I graduated college that I at least gave real estate a shot. I received my license three months after graduating from the University of Georgia and experienced some early success due to my personality and huge family in and around Nashville.

By 2007, the real estate market was starting to waver, and I realized my results were leveling off. A local lender and CORE coach told me of his success from this national coaching program and asked me to attend my first Summit in California. I reluctantly attended.

At this Summit, I watched Rick Ruby yell about making money, saving money, and changing the planet. As many do, I thought he was a little crazy the first time I met him. The principles he and his coaches taught were not ground breaking; they were the same basic principles I had been taught when I started in the real estate business, but he had one key ingredient I was missing: accountability.

As I prepared to leave the Summit with a head full of ideas and changes I would make to my business, my ego got in the way, and I thought, "I can do this on my own," and I didn't sign the intent form. Once back in Nashville, two local CORE students asked me why I hadn't signed the form, and I explained that I could do it on my own. They both expressed the lack of accountability in my business and that I wouldn't be able to do it. I hate to admit it, but they were right.

As the next Summit approached in Atlanta, I realized I had quickly fallen back into the bad habits I was trying to kick after the last Summit. I signed up for the Atlanta Summit with a new mindset: I would listen to coaches and see how the CORE could help my business.

Once in Atlanta, I met Reeta Casey, and she helped me realize I needed to stay ahead of the rapidly changing market and get my business in order. My business was broken, I had no balance in my life working 70-plus hours per week, and I had recently gotten married. I had to change what I was doing. The Summit concluded in the similar fashion as the previous Summit, and as before I didn't sign the intent form out of fear; fear of the monthly cost, fear of the massive change that would occur in my business and life, fear of the unknown. At the final dinner, Reeta sat with me and asked about my experience and what I was going to change, assuming I had signed the intent form. Once she found out otherwise, she asked, "Why not?" I used every excuse in the book as to why I didn't sign the form, and once she overcame every objection I had, I realized, I had to sign up. Thank you Reeta for influencing the best business decision I have made in my 11-year career.

Rick, Reeta, and Todd accepted me as the "charity case student" as I didn't make enough money to qualify as a student, but I promised Rick that I would make it and make them proud. In my first couple semesters, I fought change and saw minimal differences in my overall numbers, which became frustrating. I even contemplated quitting until I realized that The CORE would only work if I surrendered to the coaches and accountability.

My first big surrender was to Dayton Schrader, and finally committing to attend Rapport Leadership I. What a breakthrough! Rapport helped me realize I was the only thing holding me back from being a great real estate agent. I needed to get out of my own way and change. Consider the ceiling broken. That semester I fully surrendered, broke the $150,000 taxable income mark, and paid off the $30,000 in debt I had accrued prior to joining The CORE.

With one mindset broken, Todd Scrima began teaching me the art of delegation and maximizing my green time (money-making time). In the next two years, I had my best years EVER (to that point), in the recession of 2009 and 2010, making $165,000 and $189,000, respectively. I built a team to support me and take great care of my clients, but I was still missing something. I was thinking as a real estate agent and not as a business owner.

As a real estate business owner with a company generating over $300,000 in gross commissions, I learned I needed to be clear on everyone's job roles. I no longer needed to be in the files or concerned with anything that didn't generate leads or close deals. With the help of The CORE, I leveraged my team members' strengths to secure large channel accounts and hone in on a sales style that fit me and my market. The CORE taught me how to qualify and close business partners, as well as leverage my database and the vast amount of contacts I had made over my career. In other words, go deeper with the people I already knew.

With a new business mindset and an amazing team to support me, I truly broke through, finally breaking the $250,000 mark in 2012 making $287,000. With the added business came the need to grow my team, and in 2013, my coaches helped me hire my first RP2 (buyer's agent). I was generating 50-plus leads per month and I couldn't service that many leads on my own. I hired an RP2 who took over the advertisement piece of my business (sign calls, Internet leads, etc.) and helped me to focus on the warm leads from my family, friends, past clients and business partners.

By focusing on the people that know, love, and trust me, I learned the power of deep relationships and that a small, personal gift can last a lifetime. In 2013, we threw parties, happy hours and pampered the people who had shown me the most love and helped me build the real estate business I had built. Who knew that growing a business could be so challenging but FUN? That year truly showed me the sky's the limit as I posted another record year, making $489,000, and more importantly, giving away over $20,000. Although the numbers are great, the biggest honor of that year came in December.

After the November Summit in 2013, six years after attending my first Summit in California, Rick called me to inform me that I had been voted as one of the next real estate agent coaches. What an honor! To have the peers I have looked up to and learned so much from accept me as one of their own was the most amazing feeling I have felt in business. Being a coach would give me an opportunity to learn more from not only the other coaches, but from the students I would be coaching.

Thanks to Rick Ruby and The CORE, my now family of four is on a path to financial freedom and truly changing the planet.

# Hunter Marckwardt

## Lender Coach

**Location**: Alamo, California

**Started with The CORE**: July 2010

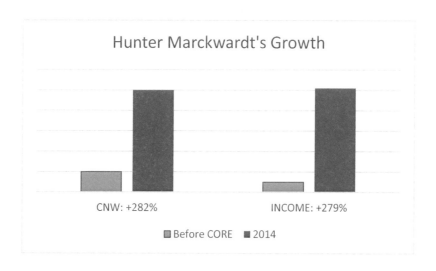

Hunter Marckwardt's Growth

CNW: +282%          INCOME: +279%

■ Before CORE   ■ 2014

# Hunter Marckwardt

My journey began after graduating from University of Arizona with a degree in finance. I was eager to start interviewing with the top investment banks in San Francisco. I was excited to jump in head first. I had grandiose visions of walking through downtown San Francisco with my new suit, new shoes, brief case, coffee in hand, being important and helping my company figure out some of the top financial problems of the day. I used a few different connections to get in front of these companies, but always seemed to get pawned off to some junior person for the interview. Most of these memories were not memorable, but one interview did stand out. This junior investment banker had to interview me, and he literally had not left the office from the day before.

He said to me, "Hunter, see that office, and that office, and that office? Well, that guy went to Harvard, that guy went Wharton, and that guy went to Yale. You seem like a nice guy but you're not getting in here with a degree from the University of Arizona."

I thought, "Wow, well this sucks."

My best friend's older brother had been hired at Nextel Communications a year earlier and was showing success, although he had some previous experience before going there, which was a prerequisite for being hired. Somehow my buddy's brother convinced Nextel Management we would not let them down, and they

180

hired both of us. Everyone in sales should have had this job.

My first day at work my boss drives me to the industrial park in Benicia, California, shows me my territory, helps me do a few cold calls to see how it's done, and then we're done, training day over.

Next day I get in my car, I drive to Benicia with one of my two suits my dad was kind enough to buy, with my one pair of Allen Edmonds, and a Nextel Phone in hand. I get out there at 8:00 in the morning and over the radio comes my boss. Screaming at the top of his lungs he says, "Hunter, I want you to get out there and kill that pig, kill that pig, hit 'um, hit 'um, bang bang, kill that pig…"

That was his way of saying, "Go make a sale!!" The first four months of my job, I cold called and cold called, every single day. If I found out from a concrete contractor's secretary that he was only in the office at 6:00 a.m., I'd be there at 6:00 a.m. I saw very few results in the first three months, but in the fourth month I was 327% above quota. My buddy was a county over doing the exact same thing. In our first year we both made Presidents Club and were the #7 and #9 producing sales reps of 2000 for Nextel. Best first job experience one could ask for.

In hindsight, the biggest lesson I learned from Nextel was that successful people do what unsuccessful people are not willing to do. I didn't know cold calling sucked, I just did it, every day. My peers, who were older and with more experience, also brought some bad habits with them, which included a disdain for cold calling. In any sales job you have to be willing to cold call, at least some of the time.

The other lesson I learned was how critical it is to have a supportive boss. My boss was crazy nuts, but he supported me in everything I did. He fought for me internally, and he would go out in the field with me to support, to cold call, to help close deals; he was with me the whole way versus sitting in an ivory tower telling me what to do. It's actually one of the things I love so much about The CORE is that we're all willing to do the same things we have others doing.

Nextel lasted three great years, but I decided I needed my next challenge, which was software. After a couple of mishap companies, I wound up at a small startup named Contivo. This was, in fact, the big leagues. My executive staff and others had just taken companies public and were literally worth a fortune. I literally had no business being in this job. I'll skip the story about how I got it, but I was nervous as all hell, I was young, and I knew the company was looking at me like, "Remind me what Hunter's experience is in software and what he's doing here?"

When you're dealing with startups, you're very tight with the board, the executives, and the whole company overall. There is also huge pressure to produce. Here I was selling a software application that I had absolutely no clue as to what it did, what problem it solved, how, and/or why. Within three weeks of starting work I had to do a presentation in Texas to 20 Enron people. Upon my return home, one of the executives called one of our board members (who was the CEO of a Fortune 50 company) and said, "The sales engineer is good, but your sales guy is an idiot."

That message went from board member, to CEO, to VP of sales, to me. Within 30 days of the job I was on the chopping block. My boss told me our CEO was coming to watch me present to a potential client, and if he didn't like it, I'd basically be driving home from the meeting. Fast forward three years, I stuck with it, I saw three CEOs go before me, four VPs of sales, and 23 sales people. I ended up closing the biggest deal the company had ever seen to help with the HP/Compaq merger. Everything happens for a reason. I learned more about myself in those three years than any other time. I had the opportunity to work with some of the best of the best, and many are friends to this day. I actually refinanced the entire executive staff when I left to go into the mortgage business, as well as half the company.

The lesson learned here for me is you never burn bridges. Those guys knew I worked my butt off for them, they also knew I was never in my comfort zone even if I was "okay" at doing it. Long-term relationships are built on trust and respect. Some of the biggest relationships I have in the mortgage business today with real estate agents and financial advisors were provided by the referrals of my executives at Contivo.

My ending with Contivo came when I was driving home one night, stuck in Silicon Valley traffic for 90 minutes and thinking to myself, there is more to life than this. When I arrived home, I told my wife I had to do something else, which she agreed with 100%. As much as I loved the people I worked with, the job itself was killing our relationship, my confidence, and me.

Mortgage business here I come. I went to work for a small brokerage in Danville my first three years in the business, from 2002-2005. Having larger loan amounts than the rest of the country, we were doing a lot of refinances and a few purchases. I was calling on previous relationships more so than real estate agents. My parents taught me the value of putting in a solid day, but for the first time in my professional life I didn't have to be somewhere at a particular time, nor did I have a quota, or a boss looking over me. The world is our oyster in the mortgage business, which is a blessing and a curse. We know everyone is a potential client, but how do we get to them? The first three years in the mortgage business I think I averaged three deals a month.

Of the 36 deals in a year, maybe five of them were purchases. I was making a decent living, nothing earth shattering, but I was fine with it financially. Mentally however, I was truly starting to think to myself, "This isn't very gratifying." Taking someone's interest rate down .25% as a "no cost" refinance and making a point just didn't feel that good. It's still a decent living, but if you have any desire for mental growth and development, it's not going to happen here.

After three years into the mortgage business, I had the opportunity to work for RPM, where I'm still currently. It's one of the top 10 mortgage banks in the country and has a fantastic reputation in our local market. Even with RPM, my major focus was still refinances. I shared an assistant with one other person and did pretty well. I was always in the top 20 of RPM, but never really breaking past the point of 5-10. My purchase units were still in the 15-20 a year. Then 2007-2008 happened, the mortgage meltdown, and I thought I was done, so much so that my CEO from the software days had started a new company, and I started contracting with him 2.5 days a week as his sales guy down in Palo Alto. I started doing the same thing again that was killing me and my marriage, and I knew it the moment I got in the car the first day to go down to Palo Alto.

Fast forward six months and I made the best decision I've ever made, which of course was to go to my first CORE Summit.

If you've ever heard my story, you know I hate crowds, or should I say, I hated crowds before. The idea of me getting in a room with a bunch of lenders and real estate agents and listening to some crazy guy screaming at me about how I'm doing it all wrong was as interesting to me as stabbing my eyes out. But there I was, back of the room, listening to Rick Ruby, thinking to myself "I don't want to like this guy but I do." Everything he was saying I knew to be true. I knew I didn't like what he was saying because it went against my current business plan, which was no plan, but I couldn't escape the fact that he was right.

After three days of this Summit, talking to coaches, and honestly questioning whether or not these people were full of it, my only proof point was a guy in my office who had signed up for CORE training six months ahead of me. I saw him going up the rankings in our company, from not being in the top 20 to being our #1 commissioned loan agent, so something had to be working, and these guys might not be full of it. I called my wife after the event and we discussed whether or not I should try this. We both decided I had nothing to lose. I was either going to gain momentum and succeed, or I'd likely be out of the business inside of two years. Aside from marrying my wife, joining the CORE is without question the biggest and best decision I have ever made. I'm actually proud of myself for having made it. So many times in my life I would just say "Nope, I don't need this, I'll do it alone"…only to find myself in the exact same rut a week later.

I started with Todd Scrima as my first coach, and what a way to start. I could still hide behind some refinances, but he saw through me. His ability to hold me accountable and to ask the questions that would uncover what I was and wasn't doing boggled my mind. More than anything, he helped me get my head straight. As I look back on it now, so many decisions I make today are tactical and not as emotional, where before they were all emotional. Think about your life and if you had the ability to make tactical decisions more times than not, your life would be better for it, 100% guaranteed.

One year into The CORE, I had my own LP2, was closing five to seven deals a month, and my purchase business was picking up steam. Then I was assigned to Rick Ruby as a coach. Me being the big shot I thought I was, I called Todd Scrima and announced I wanted him to be my coach again. He kindly explained that's not how the system worked and said I'd like Rick. I told him again in the nicest way possible that if I'm spending all this money, I should have a say in my coach. Within two minutes I picked up the phone to the angriest man in the world, Rick Ruby, who unkindly told me I'd be having him as my coach this semester, and if I didn't like it, I could quit…

So that was that. Rick taught me to be strong. If you can deal with Rick, and trust me, you can, you can deal with anything. He makes you stronger, he makes you better, he makes you relentless, he makes life a bunch of tactical decisions versus emotional ones. He can pound you down, but he can lift you up as much as anyone I've ever seen. I went from not wanting Rick as a coach to having my best semester in The CORE and winning the coveted blue dragon award, which is awarded to the hardest working student with the biggest results for a given semester.

Two years into The CORE I had three people on my team and things were starting to hum. I tend to be a very slow learner, I'm very stubborn, and I have had a hard time in the past, with the word SURRENDER. This word is the single most important word in The CORE. I tried, like I'm sure many before me, to use The CORE as an "a la carte menu." It doesn't work as an a la carte menu. It works only when someone fully surrenders to their coach, the plan, and their homework. I finally understood this two years in, and that's when my business took off.

After graduating, I approached Rick about being a coach, another decision I never would have made without The CORE. I had the confidence that I could do it, and I loved the idea of challenging myself to do something I've never done before and growing my experience in life. This is where I find The CORE so magical. I understand to the outside world it can appear to be some crazy cult with a bunch of high energy "believers" preaching the gospel of Rick Ruby and how to sell, but in the end, it's an organization of a bunch of positive people wanting to improve their lives, the lives of the ones they love, their clients, and the outside world. When you're fully committed, or fully surrendered, your life goes places you never would have anticipated.

Fast forward to today: I have a team now of six people, I had my best month ever with $16,600,000 last month in funded loans, and I'm loving my job and my life. I've been a coach for two-and-a-half years, and I find it to be the most gratifying job I've ever had. The thought that I get paid to help people be more successful is unbelievable. Selfishly, every time I help someone else, I'm helping myself even more. Having to practice everything I preach and stay accountable to my students has made me more accountable to my family, my church, giving, and myself.

After all this time I've realized now that our worlds at work are broken down into three important words that have huge meaning behind them: structure, accountability, and leadership. I think about those three words every single day now. I say those words every single day. I think to myself on a regular basis, "Am I being purposeful right now?" All small, simple, messages and tactics that, done over and over again, create a framework for success. I owe so much of what I've done in the past six years to The CORE. The coaches, the students, and the company are a part of my family. I wish everyone could experience what I have. It's truly an amazing thing what anyone of us can accomplish when we surround ourselves with the right people, surrender, and then hold each other accountable to be better than the day before.

# Tom Merritt

## Lender Coach

**Location:** Chicago, Illinois

**Started with The CORE:** July 2010

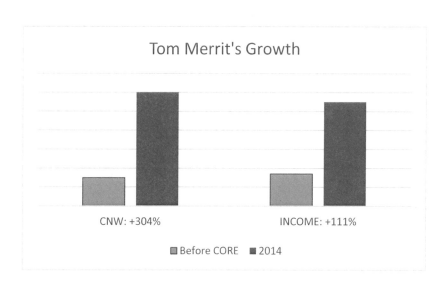

Tom Merritt's Growth

CNW: +304%    INCOME: +111%

■ Before CORE    ■ 2014

# Tom Merritt

I first heard about The CORE Training in November of 2009. A colleague of mine attended a Summit in Orlando. He raved about the experience he had, what he learned, as well as all the coaches there and what they were accomplishing in their markets. Every coach was making hundreds of thousands of dollars more than he was, and they were not working near the hours. He had submitted an application to be coached and told me I had to attend the next Summit and check it out.

By the time 2009 ended, I had closed 145 loans and made approximately $300,000, with a cash net worth of $250,000. Life was good, if you consider working 60-plus hours as a one-man show with no help or support. I was happy with my income, but felt I had hit a ceiling and needed to see how I could take that next step in my career.

I attended the Summit in May of 2010 in Scottsdale, Arizona, and after the first day, I realized I either needed to change the way I did business or find another job. The way I was running my job was not a long-lasting business model, and if I continued at that pace, I was headed towards complete burn out.

A year earlier, my eldest son was born, and I had another on the way in the fall 2010. I was not going to be able to continue working the 60-plus hours and enjoy life if something did not change. I had no structure, no defined process, no team, and was working way too much to be able to spend the quality time I wanted with my quickly growing family.

It was at the end of this Summit in May 2010 that I made the decision that would change my life forever. I signed up for coaching. After submitting the required paperwork and going through an interview with Todd and Rick, I was accepted into the coaching program.

Fast forward less than four years later and through The CORE coaching program I was able to earn over $700,000, build a team consisting of an LP1, LP2 and dialer, and in addition, start my own branch with three producing loan officers and growing. The most exciting part for me is that my cash net worth will break $1 million in 2014, and my hours have fallen to about 45 per week, enabling me to spend quality time with my friends and family.

Obviously, this did not happen overnight. The first six months were difficult as there were so many new processes, structures, and forms I had to implement into my business. I was fortunate enough to have Todd Scrima as my first coach. He was patient yet firm, and each coaching session taught me something new and challenged me in another way.

At the time, my primary sources of business were my database and financial planners, which primarily resulted in refinances. I had a couple of real estate agents that I got a few deals from here and there, but I was not in line with The CORE's principle of real estate agents, real estate agents, real estate agents. It was that initial six-month period that Rick affectionately dubbed me the "Refi King of Chicago."

From the beginning Todd preached real estate agents, and through many different homework tasks and assignments, it was apparent we were starting the task of changing the foundation of my business.

Of all the homework assignments, the most memorable assignment/challenge Todd gave to me was to call 50 real estate agents in one day and ask for an appointment.

CALL 50 REALTORS??!!!

IN ONE DAY???!!!

At that point in my career, I did not even know 50 real estate agents, let alone be able to call 50 of them. Especially in one day! I was able to complete the assignment but it took me nearly the full day. Today I call 40 real estate agents every Monday, typically in a two-hour span. How mindsets change...

The other assignment that immediately changed my business was hiring my first LP2. She came on and was tasked with putting together all my applications, gathering the necessary paperwork and coordinating between the processor and client.

Looking back, I realize that even at that point in my coaching, The CORE was setting the foundation for looking at what I was doing as a business owner and not as a sales person. My business was transforming, and ever so slowly, I was seeing the big picture of always prospecting, implementing, leveraging, and delegating.

Over the remaining year and a half of my two-year contract in coaching, I was able to really form my team and start the change of my business from database and refinances to real estate agents and purchases. By the time I graduated, I had an LP1 and LP2 and was doing about 50% purchase business and had doubled my cash net worth.

I was asked by many other students in The CORE if, now that my two-year obligation to The CORE was complete, I was going to continue. While I felt as though

I had accomplished a lot, I also felt like I was still in the beginning stages of what I now envisioned was possible in this career.

My team of an LP1 and LP2 allowed me to cut my hours while producing more as I was able to focus on the prospecting side of the business much more. My relationships continued to grow and deepen as I now started looking at my referral partners as my clients and made it a goal to "Wow" them with every deal that we did together.

Although my business continued to grow, and I had more bandwidth than I had ever had, my business was not where I wanted it to be. I had realized that there was so much opportunity, as evidenced by other CORE Members. They were setting records year after year with their growth, and I was way behind.

In talking through this with my coaches, I realized a lot about myself and the type of person I was, versus the qualities of those who grow more quickly. What I learned is that the quickest person to implement is typically the most successful, and I was slow to implement.

This "ah-ha" moment took me back to my second semester of coaching when I was paired with Scott Forman and Hunter Marckwardt. It was an amazing call, and lifelong friendships were made. It was our second semester, and we all were at approximately the same income level and team structure.

It was about this time that The CORE had just started implementing the dialer position. Scott Forman implemented quickly and hired a dialer. Hunter and I held out, waiting to see what the results looked like. About a year later Hunter hired his first dialer. For me it took three years.

Hiring a dialer changed my life in that my real estate agent meetings exploded. I started meeting with more real estate agents over the next six months than I had met with in my entire career. If I would have just surrendered earlier and implemented, who knows where I would be today. Scott is currently number one in The CORE and has more than five dialers and Hunter is in the top 10.

Lesson learned: Implement quickly.

As my journey continued, my goals and visions grew and shifted to not only being one of the best loan officers in my city, but owning and running a highly profitable branch with elite loan officers all following The CORE model.

In the summer of 2012 I started running a branch for my company and took on the challenge of not only continuing to build my business, but also recruiting and growing my new branch with loan officers with whom I could share the vision of The CORE.

With this venture came a whole new set of responsibilities, structure, and processes, but with some recruiting and vision, my branch is slowly but surely getting off the ground and providing me the opportunity to build a culture and environment that provides for many families and gives me the opportunity to accomplish goals I never thought reachable.

While I now I have come a long way in my CORE journey and hit many goals I never envisioned were possible, I also realize I have a long way to go. The CORE has given me the mindset and the knowledge that the sky is the limit and that anything is possible if you work at it. Through prospecting, leverage, delegation and quick implementation anything is possible, and whatever your goals and aspirations are, they can be achieved.

I continue to modify and change my vision and my goals, but I know I will hit them. Now it is that elusive $1 million in W2 earnings and a branch with 10 loan officers averaging 10 loans a month. Four years ago in my mind it would have been impossible. Today it's just a question of how soon I get there.

See you at the top!

# Jo Anne Johnson

## Realtor

**Location**: The Woodlands, Texas

**Started with The CORE**: January 2012

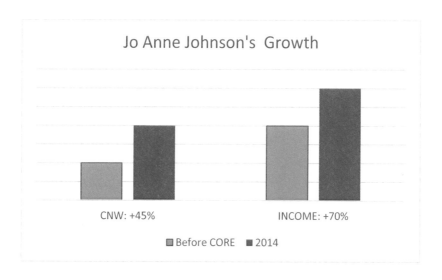

# Jo Anne Johnson

It was the summer of 2009, and my business was growing at a pretty good clip. All was good in the world, except for maybe the fact that I was burning out in only my second year as a real estate agent!

I defined customer service as being available to my client 24/7. I rationalized that, in the name of service, I was a hero if I was responding to emails at 2 a.m. to clients across the globe. I didn't realize how out of whack my life was! My husband was caught between being supportive and wondering what kind of crazy carousel I had stepped on.

At my husband's urging, I hired my first assistant in early 2010. Together, we started formatting checklists and implementing systems. Without any model or template to work from, it felt like we were building a spaceship!

Along came a lender acquaintance who wanted to partner in building our businesses with like-minded goals. I liked what he was saying and admired his forthrightness and the way he persisted over the next few months.

Slowly, my world started to change...

This lender acquaintance invited me to an event to hear Rick Ruby, his professional coach. I wasn't too familiar with professional coaches and methods. I had been introduced to a few tapes or scripts in my initial broker training and was turned off by their scripts and tactics, as they just seemed too "plastic," insincere, impersonal, and disingenuous. They seemed to lose focus from the client. So, I asked my assistant to attend in my absence. Thankfully, she was bold enough to come back and tell me what a huge mistake I had made!

When I finally attended a CORE Summit almost a year later, I was blown away by the energy in the room and the caliber of professionals. We were pounded by the inspiration to "do more and be more," profitability through accountability, to know your numbers, including your personal budget, to give until it hurts, and to surrender to your coach. The absence of egos and the culture of sharing was unbelievable. Most of all, I was amazed at the open profession of faith. How refreshing! I was in a league of mega-producing lenders and real estate agents from around the country, and they were sharing their P&Ls and personal budgets. It. Was. Unreal.

"Be true to your author." I heard that very clearly from Rick in talking about authenticity. Rick, Todd, and Reeta were not about coddling our egos. In fact, at my first lunch during the Summit, Reeta Casey told me that my struggle to grasp the value of prospecting was "between my ears." WOW. I was getting my butt kicked all over the place, and it was also apparent that they genuinely cared about my future success.

Rick's style is not for everyone. He requires honesty and accountability, effort, humility, transparency, charity, humility, and most of all, ACTION!

At all levels of CORE coaching and training, we're asked if our coaching experience has been life-changing. The answer is "yes."

I am grateful and humbled.

# Larry Montani
## Lender Coach

**Location**: Ocean, New Jersey

**Started with The CORE**: January 2011

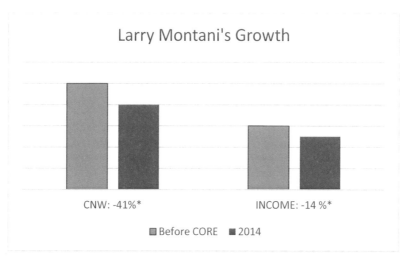

*\* Larry's numbers reflect a transition from an inflated focus on refinance business to a consistent focus on purchase business.*

# Larry Montani

Let's begin with the end in mind….

I begin the story of my journey with The CORE with one of the most powerful lessons I have learned from my father. My dad taught me to always envision where you are going to be. My journey, not unlike many of my fellow CORE students, is very incomplete but because of the structure, discipline, and accountability that has been thrust upon me by all of my coaches, I am positive my "end" game will be achieved. The biggest reason I have grown is because of one word: surrender. With that in mind, let's go back to the beginning of my story.

Upon graduating college in 1986, I was desperately in search of a job. I was so anxious to secure employment that I took the first job offered to me. I began work in June 1986 as a Marine insurance underwriter for Chubb Insurance in New York. I commuted by train to the city every day. One day I bumped into an individual who was assigned the task of opening an office to Citicorp Mortgage. While I enjoyed her company, I did not think of changing jobs, considering I had just started with Chubb Insurance. Well after only five months at Chubb, I was let go. I simply was not grasping the job and admittedly did not like it anyway. Being unemployed and candidly embarrassed, I was a lost soul. I was very frustrated and simply did not know what I wanted to do. Then, by some stroke of luck, I received a call from Citicorp Mortgage. They were looking for a clerk for the Shrewsbury office which was about to open. I jumped at the chance and started in December 1986.

While at Citicorp I began as a clerk, but was quickly promoted to account executive. This was a fancy name for processor. I managed an average of 100 loans per month and was baptized into the mortgage business very quickly. I loved what I was doing because it dealt with math and people. I achieved such great success that I was promoted to account sales executive (sales rep) and obtained the highly coveted Service Excellence Award. This award is only given to 20 Citibank/Citicorp employees annually. Boy was I psyched! I felt that I had arrived and my future was set working for such a prestigious company.

Upon receiving my award, I assumed I was going to get a big raise, which I felt was overdue and deserved. I met with the president of Citicorp Mortgage for dinner, where he honored me with a $250 bonus check. Boy was I pissed! On my train ride home I did some deep thinking and realized I needed to make a change, but what? After the disappointment of being fired by Chubb, I was scared to be unemployed. This fear resulted in me not looking for employment elsewhere because of the "security" I already had. As a result of my success, I started to become more vocal in the office for what I thought was for the benefit of my fellow employees. Well, I went from "Service Excellence Award Winner" to being on probation. While I still worked hard and did the best I knew how, I knew I needed to move on, so I did. I was hired as a sales manager for a local mortgage broker.

I worked as a mortgage broker for First Jersey Mortgage Company for nine months, and then decided I needed to be in total control of my own destiny, so I started a mortgage company with two partners only one month after my eldest son was born. The name of the company was First Interstate Financial Corp (FIFC). We were licensed mortgage bankers located in a small executive suite office with only one employee. I wrote my first loan for my company on October 16, 1989.

From there my firm had massive growth, and of course, changes. Our biggest year was in 2003 where we closed $1.6 billion – yes, billion. Life on the surface was great, but I was working too many hours, had limited structure, was frustrated with my partners, and to top it off, my wife had breast cancer. Bottom line, I felt I had a void I needed to fill, but just like in 1986, I was not sure how.

As the market began to change massively in 2008, so did my company. We were fighting the fight to keep things alive, but between poor money management, heightened aggravation with my partners, and the ever-glaring pile of "buy backs," we were truly up against it. We made one bad decision after another, which cost me hundreds of thousands of dollars.

In May 2010 we decided to hitch our wagon with a firm out of Pennsylvania who had capital and needed sales. It appeared to be a great match, but the ink was not even dry when they started to change everything. It was a total disaster. On top of this, the entire industry was starting to turn the loan process upside down. So between the massive guideline changes and the new company's inefficiency and inability to perform, we were falling apart. Our referral partners and clients were losing confidence in us every day, and try as we might, it just was not getting better. The stress and anxiety was unimaginable, and although I remained optimistic, the reality was the business we had built had crumbled, and I had gone from being an owner to a loan officer with only a few personal team members.

It was at this point I decided I needed to get away and clear my head. I went to a conference in Orlando, Florida, titled "Mortgage Revolution." I went primarily to hear the key note speaker. At the break after the key note speaker was finished, I asked a dear friend of mine what break out session I should go to next. He directed me to Rick Ruby, whose topic was "How to Run a Branch." I found him to be incredibly direct, which was something I enjoyed. I was intrigued by his speech so much that I chased him out of the conference room to speak to him personally. Hard to believe, he was short and abrupt, but I was persistent and asked if I could speak to him further. He said, "Call my office," and walked away. I was speechless but figured, what the heck?

Upon returning to my office the next week, I called him and scheduled a teleconference call. The call was intense, and he was totally in control – something which was foreign to me. His questions were intriguing, and I found myself wanting to meet him face-to-face. I scheduled a site visit at his North Carolina office.

I arrived early on a Friday morning in September 2010. My expectation was that I would arrive at a very professional office building. Boy was I wrong. It was a rented house, and when I knocked on the door, I was greeted by two very large dogs. I thought to myself, "What am I doing here?" I proceeded to spend the entire day with Rick and was once again intrigued. He spoke about time management, lead conversion, budgets, and so much more. Bear in mind, I had never truly focused on any of these topics in my LIFE. After a very long and interesting day, I left for home. Upon returning to the office, I decided to sign up for my first Summit, which was held in Austin, Texas, in November. At the end of the Summit, I put in my application to become a student, and thankfully, I was accepted.

Let the games begin...

I began my first semester in January 2011. To say I was lost would be an understatement. I was clueless about the forms, and my lack of executing them made me feel paralyzed. When I started to figure them out, I became so very upset because I realized what a mess I was with both my business and financial life. I thought I was trying; the reality was I was only halfway committed, and as a result, I was seen as a very poor and disruptive student. To make matters worse, my partners and I were at odds, and my branch was hemorrhaging cash due to overspending. Despite these challenges, and despite being in a depressed state, I never missed submitting my homework on time and participating in every coaching call.

Realizing my relationship with my partners was toxic and unhealthy, I officially parted ways with them in November 2011 and joined another firm. It was at this time that Rick Ruby was assigned to be my next coach. He was firm but fair to me and never pulled any punches. He tried to break me, but I refused to give up. It was at this time that things finally started to turn around, primarily because my attitude was improving. I went from feeling sorry for myself to taking on a "can do" attitude. I dug my heels in and worked even harder.

Unfortunately, my results were not reflective of my effort.

Then, in July 2012, I received my third coach, Jim Reed. Jim's calm demeanor and passion to teach was very apparent. Once again, I re-committed myself to be the best student I could be. I improved on my execution and slowly started to see results. I felt I was finally on the comeback trail. I not only did my homework, but studied it as well.

My effort paid off in the spring semester of 2013 when I won my first Blue Dragon. This was so important to me because it represented that I had turned my business around and that I belonged. I was really proud of myself but knew there was still a lot of work to do. In my sixth semester with The CORE, I was assigned to Shayla Gifford. Her incredible spirit and humility was inspiring, to say the least. I fed off her energy and really embraced the CORE model even further. Things were gelling, and I was very excited. She honored my efforts with my second Blue Dragon in November 2013.

Fast forwarding to my eighth semester, I was assigned to Scott Forman. His generosity in providing me the systems and techniques to grow have not only helped me personally but also my entire team. He is a true leader, but more importantly, a great friend who has inspired me to surrender at an even higher level. Also, he has not only helped me to understand the often-used but many times misunderstood word of "accountability." Through Scott, I have learned not only what I want done, but also how and when, for the benefit of my group. Lastly, through Scott's mentoring, I have finally relaxed and truly know what I want to do in business to be happy.

Well as you can see from the above, I really needed to make many changes, and by embracing the word "surrender," I continue to do so. The best part of being a member of The CORE is the fact that I have concentrated on and have become a better husband, father, friend, and boss. The joy I have had by giving back what I have learned cannot be measured. This is where I have been most successful in the last four years. Also, I have developed amazing friendships with my fellow students, coaches, and the entire staff at The CORE, something I deeply cherish. The love and support of everyone I have come in contact with drives me to succeed, and more importantly, give back.

When asked to memorialize my journey, one of the questions pointed to me was, "What are your dreams for the future of your life/business and how will The CORE help?"

My dreams are simple. I want to help everyone I come in contact with, and the best way I know how is to not only define the word, but in fact, teach them how to "surrender." This will now and forever be my life's mission, and I look forward to doing it with the help of my family and The CORE. Simply put, I will make sure they begin with the end in mind.

And now you know the rest of the story.

# Molly Nadeau-Peterson

## Lender

**Location:** Plymouth, Minnesota

**Started with The CORE:** July 2014

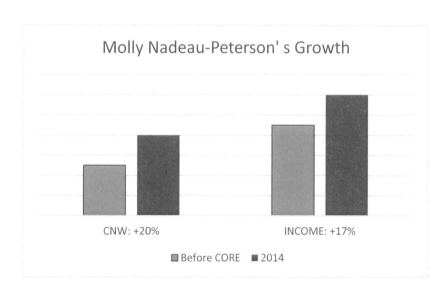

Molly Nadeau-Peterson' s Growth

CNW: +20%     INCOME: +17%

▪ Before CORE  ▪ 2014

# Molly Nadeau-Peterson

I was introduced to The CORE by a fellow LO in my company. He was bossy and mean to his staff. He didn't accept responsibility for anything, and he gave orders, blaming it on The CORE. When asked by my boss if I would participate in a pilot program with The CORE, I said, "I will never do The CORE. It's not really my style."

My boss assured me I would appreciate this guy named Rick and asked me to try it anyway. In May 2012 we were a group of 15 Watertstone LOs on a half hour call with Rick Ruby every two weeks. The commitment was to be six months. By month four, there were five of us had left, and I loved it! Nobody ever talked to me the way Rick did. I had no idea how broken I was. I had no idea how far other LOs had taken their careers. I didn't know a loan office could net 1 million dollars on a W-2! If she could do it, so could I! I didn't know there were live-out-loud Christians in this industry! At the time I was averaging five loans per month and 90% refinance with three real estate agents that closed three to five loans with me per year.

I closed $12 million in 2012 and $17 million in 2013. I hired my first LP2, and she is still with me today. I started calling on real estate agents, and I met with any human with a real estate license I could get in front of. This led to me becoming a 90% purchase LO today.

Fast forward to the 1.5 program with Jen Hernandez. I was starting to manage my time better and delegate a little more. I hired my first LP1 (she is also still with me). I started calling on builders, builders, and more builders. We were supporting seven builders and 10 models in the spring and fall "parade of homes" of 2014. Now, 30% of my purchase business is new construction.

In May of 2014 I begged Courtney at The CORE to go to my first Summit. While hanging out with The CORE students and coaches during the off times and being the study-buddy in the front at each class, I discovered "my people." I made $215,000 (short of the $250,000 minimum) on my W-2, so I recruited Brian Kludt and Andy Burton to put in a good word to Rick for me. I sent Rick gifts and notes and stalked him to allow me to pay him $2,300 per month. I was accepted based on Hunter's interview notes and my bribes.

My first semester with Greg "The Karate Kid" Gale was good. I was impatient to get to the money-making assignments. We spent a lot of time on forms (mine were far from perfect). My teammates had major changes and hard things happen in life, and it brought a real human aspect to what we do.

The November 2014 Summit brought confirmation for Lisa Wells and me to work together in her new space. My team and I moved on December 1, 2014, and it was a relatively smooth transition. My team is growing by leaps and bounds in their skill sets as a result of working close and learning from Lisa's Jedi Master Mortgage Team. I couldn't imagine a bigger blessing for our careers. I ended 2014 with 102 units and $257,000 on my W-2. We hit higher volume with more consistency from June through November that year.

Now in my second semester, Scott "The Patriot" Oliver has given his commitment to encourage, push, and guide me to hitting my goals of converting three whales with three deals each by the Summit in May 2015. We have our work cut out for us.

This journey has been exciting and scary and very uncomfortable. Oh, I almost forgot – I saved $40,000 in my first year with The CORE. I have never saved so much money in any year of my life. I have given more than I have EVER given to church and charity! That feels so good. I thank God for The CORE and its leaders and staff every day!

# Steve Kaer

## Realtor Coach

**Location**: Lake Oswego, Oregon

**Started with The CORE**: July 2008

# Steve Kaer

My journey with The CORE started in the spring of 2007. I had been in the real estate business since the spring of 1979 and sensed that the real estate market was in for some turbulence.

By the grace of God, John Bruce, an original CORE member and one of Portland's top lenders, whom I'd never met, reached out to me by phone and said that I should go to this event hosted by The CORE. Without hesitation I responded, and by the following week I was sitting in front of Todd Scrima, thinking to myself, "This guy really understands the challenges of our business." A month later I was at a CORE Summit and immediately signed up for Level 3 coaching as the real estate and financial markets were on the verge of collapse.

This fortuitous decision proved to be one of the best decisions of my life. As the markets were collapsing I had a defined road map laid out by The CORE. I had confidence knowing that when I followed my CORE coaching I would have continued success in a market full of turmoil. Ensuring my compliance with the CORE principles is the accountability factor that adds carbon to the steel.

Seven years later, the process of completing tedious paperwork has become a ritual that gives me confidence and strength. Keeping track of my leads allows me to grow my network of clients and work for them with efficiency and purpose. This proven tactical sales model provides structure in a business that can often become chaotic.

With the guidance of The CORE, my business continued to grow throughout the financial crisis and is still growing today. I have established a team of agents that flourish in a consistently competitive market. I work hard to be each of my clients' "life-long real estate agent," and have tremendous efficiency, focus, and expertise, thanks to The CORE.

# Scott Oliver

## Lender Coach

**Location**: Portland, Oregon

**Started with The CORE**: July 2004

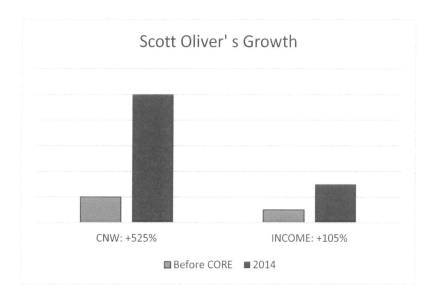

# Scott Oliver
## *"Seminar Junkie"*

In late 1989, I started selling real estate. As was the practice in those days, my broker told me that there were only three ways to make money in real estate: prospect, prospect, prospect. He told me to mail out letters to everyone I knew to tell them I was in real estate. He told me to get out the reverse directory phone book and call everyone in my "farm" neighborhood. Then he told me to knock on doors in the same neighborhood. Hmmmm....PROSPECT, PROSPECT, PROSPECT... MAIL, CALL, VISIT.

Like any logical young real estate agent, I didn't follow his advice. I went to a seminar instead. Lucky for me, it was a sales training seminar with Tom Hopkins as the lead speaker. He was a pioneer in real estate agent training. I had no money when I heard about the seminar – so like any smart real estate agent, I charged the $250 admission fee on my credit card.

I sat in the front row. I have always sat in the front row. Back in school I used to do it. I think the other kids thought I was doing it to be the teacher's pet. The truth is, then and now, I don't see so well – even with glasses. As a little kid, I couldn't see the writing on the chalk board. What I learned was if you get close to the teachers, you cannot goof around – you have to pay attention.

Being front and center watching Tom Hopkins teach the art of sales was hypnotic. You could see every nuance. When he got fired up, you could see him spit while he preached. All the while, he was smooth, confident. He taught technique, style, and individualism. But in the end he taught: MAIL, CALL, VISIT... PROSPECT, PROSPECT, PROSPECT. Hmmmm.

The true end result was that I was hooked – and not on sales – I HAD BECOME A SEMINAR JUNKIE!

That said, I did some of the work, too. Nearly every day, I implemented a new system or technique. I held open houses, called the neighbors, tried different closing techniques, and walked the neighborhood with flyers. And then I got lucky and landed my first "whale": A builder selling 50 houses a year visited one of my open houses – and, after some face-to-face time – I listed all of his houses. For the next five years, all I did was sell new construction.

For five years, I lived, breathed, and ate real estate. I was working 70-80 hours a week, and for the first time in my life, I was making enough to own a decent house and a nice Honda Accord. In that same time, my two kids were born and started to grow. One day I came home and realized that my son had grown two or three inches taller, was pulling himself up and getting ready to walk. I had missed all those changes; I couldn't even remember seeing him crawl.

On another day I was late getting home from presenting an offer to the builder. My wife's grandmother was really sick. Things were going poorly for her, and my wife really wanted to get over and see her. When we showed up, it was too late. Molly's grandmother was gone – Molly would never see her again. My tardiness had cheated her of that moment.

The truth set in: I had chosen to fail my family.

Something had to change.

I HAD TO CHANGE.

By February of 1994 I stopped selling real estate. I had been recruited by a mortgage broker to come learn how to become a loan officer. After selling new construction for five years, I had loads of relationships with the local real estate agents, so I got off to a great start. First I sent off a letter to all the real estate agents who had been my favorites to work with (MAIL). Then I called to see if we could meet (CALL). I was fortunate to meet (VISIT) with 15 or so of them. For the next few years, those 15 relationships set up a great referral base that has served me for the whole of my 20-plus years in lending.

Pretty soon, I ventured off with a friend and we started our own mortgage brokerage. We did all right. The best thing was that my hours were down to around 55 a week. However, I missed the days of going to seminars, learning something new. So I started going again. I made myself a pact that I would go every six months or so to keep my skills sharp. I went to statewide conventions. I saw more sales trainers – Jim Rohn, Mark Victor Hansen, Zig Zigler, and more. Eventually, they all started to sound the same.

Just when I thought I had it all figured out, I got a postcard (MAIL) from Joe Stumpf. The heading was something like "Get your job done in less time…and have a life." Well, that was new indeed. I called to sign up for the "free half-day seminar," and they called back to remind me to come (CALL). I got there early enough to sit right up front (imagine that), virtually face-to-face (VISIT). Again, I found myself captivated. Joe is an amazing speaker. It was clear I had lots to learn; I could do more in less time. It was a new millennium, and my business was about to change, again.

Joe taught us that systems could be set up to refine marketing. We learned that relationships mattered. The best, most enthusiastic referral sources should be the people we give great service to. For three years, I attended every event Joe and his company (By Referral Only) held in our area. Some of those systems we still use today – monthly postcards (MAIL), initial presentation dialog (VISIT), weekly update calls (CALL) – and those tactics are more effective today than ever.

One day I was headed out to another Joe Stumpf event. I was busy enough that I needed a temp just to answer the phones. It turns out that the temp had just moved out here from Michigan after working for Rick Ruby, the founder of The CORE. She scoffed at me for going to a By Referral Only event. As far as she was concerned, the only event worth attending was a CORE Summit. I thought she was pretty brash, especially since it was her first day on the job.

Then the calls (CALL) and emails (MAIL) started coming. For six months straight, calls came from The CORE's office. We didn't call them dialers back then; it was just "one of Rick's sales people." Finally I broke down and said I would come to the June event in San Diego if he would stop calling me. I guess that's the power of persistence. They got me to VISIT them!

Anyone who has attended a CORE event knows that it comes close to awe-inspiring. It is precision and professionalism exemplified. Each session starts on time. The materials are spot on. The food is terrific. The topics taught are timely and presented in a manner that gives the student real tactics to act on after the event is over. The most impactful component for me then (and at every Summit I have been to since) is the quality of the people attending. There is real synergy – great teachers and great students collaborating to get better every day.

Now I work around 42 hours a week. I am on a rigid schedule of PROSPECT, PROSPECT, PROSPECT. I CALL for two hours a day. My staff and I MAIL once or twice a month to our database. We eMAIL videos every week to real estate agents, builders, clients, and others every day. I go out and VISIT real estate agent offices, and hold Lunch & Learns, Happy Hours.

Rick tells me that if it's new, it isn't true… and if it's true, it isn't new. These days I'm still a seminar junkie getting my fix every six months at The CORE Summits. I pick up great new tactics, but I work on the same old things:

PROSPECT, PROSPECT, PROSPECT by MAILING, CALLING, AND VISITING.

# Brian Pintar

## Lender

**Location: Castle Rock, Colorado**

**Started with The CORE: January 2014**

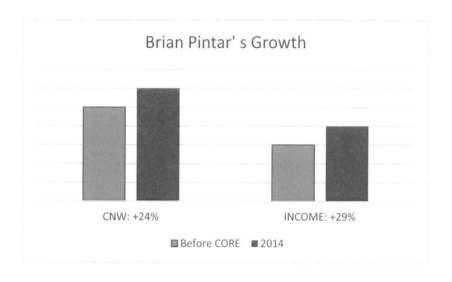

# Brian Pintar

In June 2010, my wife decided that she wanted to stay home to raise our soon-to-be two-year-old daughter and our newborn son, who was due in 60 days. Even though I had been in the mortgage industry since 1995, my wife was far and away the bread winner in the family. Her staying home would eliminate 75 percent of our household income.

We made it through the rest of 2010, closing 67 units for $179,000 in income. We struggled through the first seven months of 2011 with only 22 units closed for $62,000 in income before I was introduced to The CORE by a friend of mine. I realized I could not afford to attend the Summit, much less pay the costs of coaching. I joined the CD program, and over the next two-and-a-half years, started to implement everything I could. In the last five months of 2011, I closed 30 units and brought home $199,077. By the end of 2012, I had closed 109 units with $452,000 in income. My numbers jumped in 2013 to 115 units and $504,465 in income.

At the end of 2013, I attended the fall Summit in Arizona. At this time, the market was changing for the worse. In the fall of 2013 and spring of 2014, the average loan officer production was down more than 70 percent from the prior year. I decided to join The CORE out of fear for my and my family's future. My singular goal was to maintain my $500,000 income. I was not sure The

CORE could teach me how to make much more than that. After all, everything I did to get to the $500,000 mark was through the CORE CDs. Regardless, fear drove me to join Level 3 coaching.

I started coaching in January 2014. The first quarter was tough with regards to production. We had our worst first quarter in three years (which was still better than a lot of others in the industry). However, my coach kept pushing us to prospect, prospect, prospect. We built up a pending/approved buyer list of over 50.

Then it popped.

In May, June, and July we closed 49 units with an income of $211,900. Halfway through August, my income year to date is $360,000, and that is after closing only 22 units in the first quarter. In 2014 I am on target to make more than $700,000, of which $600,000 will have come from the last nine months of the year. In other words, I am projected to bring in on average $67,000 per month.

Finally, I have learned to manage time and delegate non-income producing tasks to my staff. This has freed time to spend with family, which is the most important thing in my life.

# Kristi Neidhardt Sargent

**Realtor**

## Location: Annapolis, Maryland
## Started with The CORE: July 2012

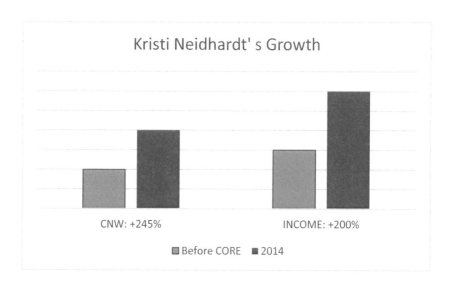

Kristi Neidhardt' s Growth

CNW: +245%          INCOME: +200%

Before CORE    2014

# Kristi Neidhardt Sargent

I had worked with a lender, Jodi, in the past when I was with a different real estate company because she was the in-house lender. To be honest, I was not impressed and rarely recommended her to clients. A few years later, she reached out to me several times to ask me to send clients her way. I turned her down time and time again.

Then she sent me a buyer – so how could I turn that down? Jodi blew me away with her service. She also won over the listing agent. After we settled, I had lunch with Jodi and asked her how and why she had changed her way of doing business. Her answer: The CORE.

She explained that it was a coaching program for both lenders and real estate agents, and she shared several CDs with me. I listened to those CDs over and over again. I implemented a few of the techniques, and my business grew, producing $6 million to $8 million. I attended one of The CORE Summits, and after seeing the kind of results the two-year program had produced for others, I applied.

I came to The CORE with about $80,000 in debt, horrible financial habits, working 80 to 100 hours a week, and a passion to never be in that situation ever again. Two years later, my taxes are paid and up to date, I have almost three months' reserves for both my personal and business expenses, and my debt is at $30,000 and falling. I am on target to hit $22 million in sales volume in 2014, and I have a team that caters to my clients and provides WOW-level service. I am working an average of 55 hours a week, I have taken three weeks off each year, and I turn off my cell phone when I am home.

I've learned that my number one client is my groom. In this two-year period, we planned a wedding and got married, he opened a restaurant, and we remodeled our home. Without The CORE to keep me focused through all that life has thrown at me, I don't even want to think about where I would be today without The CORE's guidance, expertise, and tough love.

This is only the beginning of my CORE story. With their help, I will save $2 million in cash before exiting the business, be significant in my community, and be an amazing wife, friend, and mentor.

To each of my coaches: Kendra Cooke, Reeta Casey, Dayton Schrader, and most of all, Jim Bass, "thank you" is not enough.

With great respect, gratitude and love,
Kristi Neidhardt Sargent

# Jim Reed
## Lender Coach

Location: Sacramento, California

Started with The CORE: January 2004

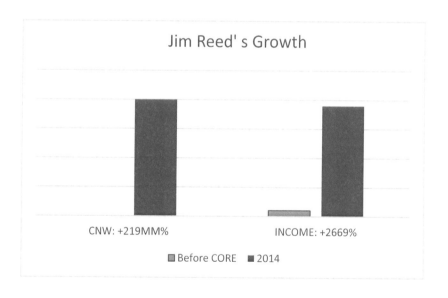

Jim Reed' s Growth

CNW: +219MM%          INCOME: +2669%

■ Before CORE   ■ 2014

# Jim Reed

My story started when I was a kid back in high school and college. I was the son of a great man, but we didn't have much money. My dad's first job was at IBM taping boxes.

I was heavily involved in track and basketball and always seemed to be attracted to leadership. My coaches always held me to a higher standard than I set for myself, and it always caused me to rise to occasion. They saw more in me than I saw in myself. Hopefully you can already see where I'm headed with this.

I remember my dad inviting coworkers over for dinner one day. After they had finished eating, they sat in the living room talking shop. My brother and I were in the kitchen eavesdropping while we ate our dessert. I remember my dad boastfully saying how much money he made, that he had finally reached six digits in income, which of course meant that he had made $100,000. I remember thinking to myself that if I could ever make $100,000, that I would be successful, too.

So fast forward to how I met Rick and The CORE.

I was roommates with Todd Scrima, owner of Summit Funding and a partner of The CORE. I met Rick at a By Referral Only event in Canada about 17 years ago. He was speaking on stage, and I remember thinking to myself, like many of you, "THIS GUY IS CRAZY!" I really didn't have any intentions of talking to him, but the next day I ran into him at the pool. The weather was nice, and Rick was holding shop like only Rick does. If you know anything about Rick Ruby, you know people follow him and hold on to every word he says.

I remember trying to sneak up close enough to hear the conversation but not wanting to be called out. All of a sudden, Rick turned, pointed to me, and said in Rick Ruby fashion, "Hey, who are you? I got a question for you. What's your batting average?"

My response obviously wasn't quick enough for him so he continued, "If I give you ten people that can qualify for a loan, how many will you get?" So I took a second to think, and then I replied, "I'd get eight or nine of them."

Can you guess what he did next? He LAUGHED! He replied, with a big grin on his face, "The best of the best could only get three or four, so I highly doubt you could close eight or nine. What I do know for sure is that you don't track your numbers."

That statement hit me like a ton of bricks. He was right. When you think about great businesses, you think about them being systematic and structured. That is the key to their success. A great business makes decisions based on facts, and at the time, the team that I was on didn't do that. We did some of it, but not all of it, and what we lacked was hurting us.

A few years later, Rick, Todd, and Reeta began their journey together building The CORE, and I was chosen to be a guinea pig. I began coaching with Rick as a team captain on Todd's team. I was making about $70,000 a year, had no money in the bank, and was $20,000 in debt. My thought process was still like the kid eating dinner, listening to his dad's conversation: If could just get to $100,000, I would be successful.

I never expected what began to happen to actually happen. I began to click with Rick, and his style reminded me of the relationships I had many years ago with my sports coaches. He began asking me this question, and still does, even to this day, "Why do I see you so much bigger than you see you?"

I remember him asking me, "Why do I know you're going to make a million bucks, and you haven't even thought of it yet?"

I remember thinking, "Oh he's just saying that. He doesn't actually believe it, but I'll just stick around anyway."

Can I tell you something? I was wrong. He did believe it.

As I continued with The CORE, I became a coach, and every year my income grew steadily. Each year he pushed me to do three things:

1. To do more business, focusing on my personal production,

2. To negotiate and renegotiate my contract when I was worth more,

3. To save.

Those are the three biggest things he's done for me in addition to helping me with my personal life.

The one thing I've seen constantly in this business concerning top producers is the "roller coaster ride" of production. Rick pointed it out in my own life. It happens because it's such an emotional thing, but that's what The CORE has helped me do – to take the emotion out. It's no longer emotional, it's tactical. If you want more business, you have to do more activity. If you want a lot more business, you have to do more of the right activity. The CORE has helped me focus on the right activity year after year, and as I've continued to do it, I've developed the skills to be better. That is what has propelled my income.

The ability to save money is based on a change in the way you think about savings and the way you think about spending. I used to think spending was a reward for my hard work. The CORE has taught me that my savings is actually a reward for my hard work, that one day I won't have to work. Now I probably always will, but one day I won't have to. The best feeling in the world is to see that day approaching more and more rapidly.

The second part of the savings equation that Rick had personally challenged me in is giving. Without his influence, I'm not sure I would have ever given away money. I would have missed out on what it feels like to help other people.

For me, The CORE has become a fraternity of people that achieve at a high level. It has given me a healthy place to compete and brag about things that matter, things like how much money we've given away and how we are "changing the planet" rather than what car we drive or the size of the house we own. I don't see that in other sales organizations or business cultures. Trust me, I've looked around. I just don't see the authenticity that I see in The CORE.

That is the word that comes to mind when I think about my friend and mentor, Rick Ruby: authentic. He walks the walk and talks the talk, but WALK comes first. He teaches us how to build our businesses and he builds his own.

That peer group is what my journey has been all about. I have matured from a kid who thought six figures was virtually unattainable, to a man who earns seven figures and has seven figures in the bank. It's a journey that I never thought I'd be so lucky to experience. Now I feel a responsibility to take people on the same journey.

In closing, The CORE has given me a peer group that keeps me challenged, grounded, and focused on the right things. When it's all said and done, that's what makes me a better husband, father, employer, and friend.

# Linda Rudd

## Lender Coach

Location: San Antonio, Texas

Started with The CORE: July 2010

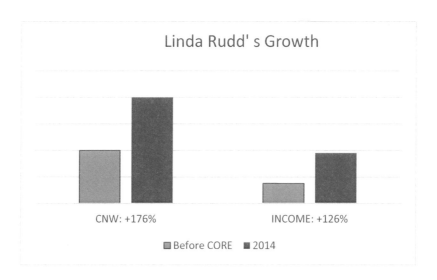

# Linda L. Rudd, CFP

I am broken...

Having been in the mortgage and lending industry for 25 years, it would seem logical to expect at this point I have it all figured out and life is easy. I am even one of the fortunate ones who have always embraced learning, coaching, and self-development. Always a student and approaching my business as a business, I excelled early and consistently. Success was awesome, hitting my peak production of $75 million and close to 500 units in 2003.

It was so awesome that I convinced myself that I was "all that" and went into business on my own with two partners and opened a net branch. The realization quickly set in that it was much more than I had ever anticipated owning and running a branch. Oh, did I mention it was right before the global meltdown of the mortgage industry?

From 2006 to 2009 my business continued to decline as banks were failing and the industry continued to contract. Thank goodness we sold our net branch to Countrywide after having worked tirelessly for 18 months (without pay).

I ran a branch for a year and then made a couple of moves to stave off failing banks. It felt like trying to run ahead of a tidal wave.

In the midst of it all, I was blessed to finally become pregnant and have an amazing daughter, the blessing of our life. I came back from maternity leave to my employer being seized by the Feds. I was inches away from stepping out of the industry altogether. It felt like total despair professionally.

Finally, at the end of 2009 I decided to reach out to my long-time rival, who happened to own Legacy Mutual Mortgage, Dan Diepenhorst. I can vividly remember the day, sending the email to Dan asking if he would like to visit over coffee. He replied immediately, and we had coffee and talked for a couple of hours. Ten days later I was at Legacy! Starting from scratch after having lost most all of my key relationships was hard, probably the hardest thing I have done in my career. I was embarrassed and angry about having to work so hard. I remember asking myself, "How did I get to this point?" After so many years I should have been set.

*My first Summit...*

In May of 2010 I had the good fortune to be introduced to The CORE by Dan. The philosophies of The CORE were and are a fundamental foundation at Legacy. At that time all new loan officers accompanied Dan to The CORE Summit on him for the first time. I have been coached off and on all throughout my career. I SWORE I would not sign up and was in no way interested in coaching at that time. Those two-and-a-half days forever changed my life in ways that I continue to discover and explore daily. I was so emotionally overcome by the message and gained complete clarity that what I needed was the accountability The CORE delivers. I signed my letter of intent that Friday night for coaching. Fortunately, Rick took me in and has become someone I hold dear both in business and in life. The CORE is my family now.

*The lessons learned (and learning)…*

**Embrace The Grind**. No matter how well I do and how much I close and make, the grind will always be my daily routine. I was of the belief that at some point I would "arrive," and from then on the heavy lifting would be over. There really is no magic to the steps to success. Most of the time it is not sexy or cool. It is doing the same things over and over and over. The CORE has provided extreme clarity on the necessary tasks and holds me highly accountable for execution. Knowing what to do is the easy part. The accountability I get from my coaches is the hard love delivery that I want and need.

**Never Stop Prospecting**. No matter what, referring partners come and go. It might be the smallest relationship, but it might be the largest! So many of us think we have a multitude of "great" relationships. I remember doing my first account pyramid and really looking at the numbers, only to discover I really only had a handful of real accounts (as defined as four or more closings per year). Again, I was embarrassed and angry – how could this be? By focusing on the tasks (and not the emotion), I have established a healthy number of relationships and added to them consistently. I love the challenge of getting a new referring partner and knowing I am at the top of my game when it comes to closing. Why? Because I LOVE to prospect, again thanks to The CORE fundamental of "never stop prospecting."

**Surrender!** Everyone takes some time to surrender to The CORE philosophies and structure, some longer than others. The system is time-tested and proven to work. For a while, I personally put a filter over the systems by deciding what I really wanted to do and what I did not. I convinced myself that I could be the judge of what to implement and when. Thus, I am not in the top ten (YET) of The CORE family. The more I surrender and embrace, the more my results reflect it. I still have a long ways to go but will never give up. I think that is the biggest "ah-ha" is that anything and everything is possible if you never give up trying.

**Life is full of obstacles and tragedies**. It is our choice as to whether it is a speed bump or a brick wall. I have heard Todd say this so many times over my four years in The CORE. I told him recently that you never know how and when you are going to impact someone. In June of this year, my father died very unexpectedly and tragically. Having grown up in a small family and having lived a very blessed life, I can share that at the age of 48 I had experienced very little personal loss in my lifetime. When this happened, it was like that message was playing in my head as I was dealing with my emotions, helping my mom, staying strong in front of my five-year-old daughter, husband, team and clients. I believe firmly that the idea that while I was not in control, but that I was in charge of my reactions was my first thought and guiding force through the tragedy. For me, the CORE family has been a source of great strength in a way I had never imagined. It is of great comfort to know there is a bond unspoken but felt on a daily basis.

The CORE is my extended family, my motivation, and my support system that keeps me grounded, and at the same time, propels me to heights previously not imagined possible. I love them, The CORE, and can't imagine life or business without them.

# Phil Puma

## Realtor Coach

**Location**: Cornelius, North Carolina

**Started with The CORE**: January 2013

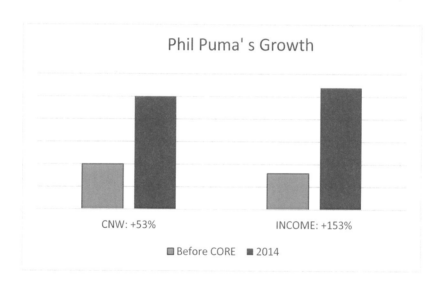

# Phil Puma

I am often asked, "So what made you become a real estate agent? Why did you choose to open your own company versus working for one of the huge firms?"

These are great questions, and up to a few years ago, I could not answer them definitively. However, I can now.

So the next question is, "Why? Why can you answer them now?"

And I say, "Great question! Let me tell you why. Let me tell you my story..."

In looking back to my college days, I never dreamed of being a real estate agent or owning my own business. After graduating from college in 1996, I moved to North Carolina from New York. I was quite naïve and thought I would land an awesome job making lots of money. However, I was wrong. After moving to a new town with little to no connections, I quickly realized how difficult things could be.

I knew I wanted to be in sales but didn't know what field. How did I know this? Well, during my last summer of college I applied for a position to sell advertisements to local businesses for the student guide. When interviewing for the job, I was handed a watch and asked, "Here, sell me this watch." I took the watch and proceeded to sell it to him. I didn't think much of it, but took the watch and began my pitch as to why this was the watch for him. It felt natural, comfortable. At the end of the pitch, the person interviewing me said, "Sold!" The job was mine. I sold out the advertising space in record time. Sales was for me.

My first "real" job was working for a consumer financing company, making loans to individuals. In doing so I realized that I liked lending, especially real estate lending. I was intrigued by the real estate market, so I went into mortgage lending and loved it! I continued down the lender path for next several years. In 1998, my wife – fiancé at the time – was working for a local bank and managed all of the REO properties. She was working closely with local real estate agents to sell the bank-acquired properties, many residential. To assist with her own understanding of real estate transactions, she decided to get her real estate license. I found myself extremely interested in what was transpiring on these properties the bank was selling, the gains, the losses, the market conditions. My interest, perhaps now an obsession, with the real estate market continued to grow, but began shifting toward the buying and selling market.

Needless to say, shortly after she obtained her license and we flipped our first investment property, I knew I wanted my license. My plan at first was to continue to be a full-time lender. I still loved the lending side but wanted to start doing some real estate deals on the side. By this time, I had built up a small network of business and personal contacts. Business was going well, referrals were coming my way for mortgages, so why not for real estate?

Shortly thereafter, referrals for home purchases starting streaming in as well. Things were good. My passion for real estate continued to shift toward helping people buy and sell homes and away from lending. In 2003, I went for it and opened my own real estate company! Things were going great! The real estate industry was on fire and business was booming. Mortgage brokerages were opening up left and right, so I thought, "Hey, with my background in lending, I should open a lending company as well!" So I did. I brought on a handful of agents and lenders and things were going great UNTIL the mortgage meltdown hit.

Whoa! What was happening?

One by one, my loan officers and real estate agents left. They needed to make a living and business was scarce. The industry was changing overnight. The new rules and regulations were daunting, so I decided to shut down the mortgage brokerage and go back to being an independent real estate agent, just me, myself, and I.

The market was tough, lending was tight, buyers were weary, sellers were underwater, but I still had my network, my integrity, and most importantly, my passion. I was going to be successful. I was going to persevere. I was raised in a blue collar household, and my father worked long hours in a steel mill to earn money to raise our family. He taught my brothers and I to not be afraid of hard work, but to embrace it and never give up. Push through the pain, the sweat, and the tears. I knew what hard work was, and I was not afraid of it.

So I dove in, worked hard, and began to build back my business. By 2011, I was back to closing a lot of business, but all I was doing was working. At this point, a typical work week consisted of more than 75 hours, getting home after my children were asleep, and leaving in the morning before they woke up. My wife often joked, "I am a single mom with two incomes."

One day I received a call from a woman named Courtney with some company called The CORE. She left me a voicemail explaining why she was calling. To be honest, I half listened to the message and deleted it. I proceeded to get one message after another from her. I remember thinking, "Wow, she is persistent," but I left it at that. I just didn't have the time to return her call.

The day came when she caught me on the phone. Once she said her name, I decided to talk, because I knew she would keep calling. I assumed this call would be just like all of the other sales calls, trying to sell something I neither needed nor had time for. I tried to get off the phone as soon as possible and just said, "Okay, send me the CDs." I had accomplished my immediate goal of getting off the phone and onto some real work.

The first CD arrived; and I tossed it into some pile of non-essential mail and went on with my work. However, something kept drawing me back to the CD. Every time I was looking for something, this CD would appear. So I stopped and looked at it.

"Hmm, it is about time management." I remember saying to myself, "Just listen to it – you need help."

So I did, and I am grateful I did. It was the first step to a new stage in my life, a much desired one. Courtney, thank you for your persistence. I am truly indebted to you.

I cannot recall how many times I listened to that first CD. I played it over and over. I heard the message, I needed it, and I wanted it. It was speaking to me. I wanted to implement these changes, but I was struggling. Courtney continued to follow up with me periodically. I now looked forward to her calls and the next CD.

One day she told me she was going to set me up on a call with Rick Ruby. I said, "Sure that sounds great!" At this point I knew Rick was the founder and one of the owners of The CORE, and I enjoyed the CDs, so why not speak with Rick. I was excited and looking forward to the call. Needless to say, I will never forget that first call. "Wow!" was all I could say.

Once again, Courtney followed up with me to ask about the call with Rick and my thoughts on the coaching program. I remember thinking, "I don't need a coach. I am a great real estate agent, I know what I am doing, and I am closing $10 million a year, so why would I need a coach?" Plus Rick was way too harsh and intense for me.

However, I loved the CDs so I continued on the CD program. I faithfully listened to the CDs and implemented some of the proposed structure and changes. In a short time, I began to see improvements in my business. Again, things were good from my perspective.

For some reason though, I could not get Rick Ruby out of my head. Our conversation was on replay. The things that Rick said just kept resonating in the back of my mind, along with his very loud voice. I was becoming more and more interested in Rick and The CORE. I wanted another opportunity to talk with him.

Since Rick and I live in the same town, I decided to attend one of Rick's local events. It was then I realized Rick is intense because he is so passionate about coaching. I knew I needed to speak to him one on one. I tracked him down at the local cigar shop. To my surprise, he did take the time to talk with me, discuss my business, discuss himself, and The CORE. I quickly realized that Rick really cares about helping others improve in business and all other aspects of life. He is genuine and truly wants to help others succeed. I knew this was for me, so I signed up for the next Summit.

My first Summit was amazing. I was able to see and hear for myself how many lives The CORE had touched and improved, how many individuals and businesses had gone from mediocre to sheer greatness. Seeing and hearing Rick and the others speak helped me begin to understand what The CORE is truly about.

I wanted in.

I wanted to change.

This was a euphoric moment, but also a very humbling one. I realized I was not as good as I thought. I did not have a great business model. Actually, I barely had a business model, and what I did have was broken. I worked too many hours, worked inefficiently, lacked procedures and processes, and had no work-life balance. I knew I had my work cut out for me, but I was up for the challenge and was open to being coached.

After that Summit, Rick personally coached me. During one of our early conversations, Rick asked, "How much $10-per-hour work did you do today?" I knew where he was headed. Growing up I was not only taught to work hard but also to save for the future. My approach was to do all the work myself and not have to pay someone else to do the work, in order to, in theory, save that money, and more importantly, know that it would be done right. Well, I already knew this approach wasn't working, so I listened. Rick told me, "You need to start running a business and not just be a real estate agent. You need to be a leader. You need more clients. Clients need to be catered to."

Rick showed me the value of building a team, the value of being a leader. I started slow, with an assistant and one buyers' agent. As we continued to grow, Rick told me to hire more people. Today, I have ten buyers' agents, a sales manager, an operations manager, a marketing coordinator, an executive assistant, an administrative assistant, a dialer, and two closing coordinators. My business has grown more than 30 percent year over year, clients are happier, and now I have more clients and more time to prospect. My bottom line has grown, my income has grown, and my savings has doubled. I am working fewer hours and spending more quality time with my family.

So if I made it sound easy, it wasn't. Hiring the team was not the difficult part; becoming an effective leader has been the challenge. Trust me, I work hard every day at being an effective leader, and Rick and the other coaches continue to challenge me to be better. One of the most important lessons I have learned, and continue to learn, is that I need to lead my team, delegate to them, empower them, trust in them, provide them structure, discipline and then love. This may seem insignificant, but I have gone from my staff copying me on every email to my assistant managing my inbox.

In addition to Rick's ongoing coaching, I have also had the pleasure of being coached by Dayton Schrader and Reeta Casey. Dayton challenged me to step outside of the box, to prospect business referral sources, to build these relationships, and to nurture these relationships, which in return, will lead to multiple referrals on a more regular basis. He told me to establish relationships with builders.

"Builders? No, that won't work!" I said.

I consistently told Dayton that it was too difficult to get builder business in my market – maybe it worked in his, but not mine. Dayton told me to go do it and stop making excuses. So I said, "Okay, I will do it, but you will see it is not going to work."

Yes, Dayton, I was wrong. After nine *long* months, and almost giving up several times, builder business starting coming in. So, another lesson learned: Listen to your coaches, stop making excuses, be persistent, and you will get the results. It can be done. Dayton, thank you for pushing me!

Reeta immediately focused on my database management. Well, I should say lack of management.

Over the years I had built up a huge network of friends, acquaintances, business partners, and other contacts. I had a list of people and their contact information, not a true database. Reeta taught me that my database is my life-line — it needs to be maintained and organized. It needs to be assessable, and you need to market to your clients on a regular and consistent basis. You need to be able to cater to them.

I now have a database that is worked daily in one form or another. In doing so, my clients know I care, know I am thinking about them, and so they think of me. I have more referrals! With my database in more order, I am now able to prospect more and prospect smarter. I am able to prospect to achieve my goals.

One of my current goals is to break into the luxury market and raise my sales price. Reeta has mastered this market, and with her ongoing guidance, I will to. Thank you, Reeta!

So here I am now. As of October 2014, I have already closed $55 million in sales, and I am on pace to close $65 million. I am working around 55 hours a week, have drastically increased my net worth, have a more balanced life, I work out daily, and attend Bible study and church on a more regular basis. Coaching has improved my life.

Have I achieved success, in the words of the man that has become my mentor and great friend?

My answer is "no."

Rick always says when we feel that we have arrived at the top and there is nowhere else to go, we fall. Therefore, we need to continue to strive to be better every day. I know I am nowhere near the top. I still have a lot of room for improvement, but I have a vision, I have a plan, and I have the support of a network of amazing people that are dedicated to helping others succeed.

Through Rick, I also have come to know Roy Mason, Rick's spiritual leader. Through listening and speaking with Roy, I truly understand that things happen for a reason, through the love and grace of God. God has a plan for all of us. So now, more than 12 years into my real estate career, I can give those questions a definitive answer.

Why?

Because I now know that being a real estate agent and owning my own business was meant to be. It was part of the plan. It was meant for me to meet Rick and be part of The CORE, to embrace and live their values. I look forward to becoming a better leader, husband, father, businessman, and add to that now, a coach, a mentor and role model.

# Niki Salter

## Lender Coach

**Location**: San Antonio, Texas

**Started with The CORE**: January 2011

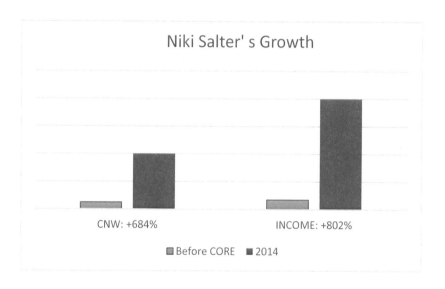

# Niki Salter

In August 2002, I was just a poor college kid in San Antonio, Texas, looking to make some money working part-time. I started as a processor in a small broker shop. After working with loan officers there for a few years, watching them and learning the ropes, I thought: "I could do that, too… and better!"

When I first started out, I was working all the time. Without any clear job descriptions or team roles, "Super Niki" would need to jump in and save the day anytime the phone rang. Let me be clear here: My team was by no means lacking in skills. What they needed was clarity and a good leader!

I was first introduced to The CORE by Shannon Silas, a real estate agent I was working with. I attended an event at Shannon's invitation, more because I wanted to make my real estate agent happy. I wasn't ready for the message. But the next time there was a speaker in town, I went just for myself, and I paid close attention. My good friend and CORE student Tom Romanello was there, and he talked to me for a while afterwards. Tom and the folks at The CORE called me and called me until I agreed to sign up for the next Summit. When I finally went to the Summit, I found the coaches, the members, and the employees to be so helpful. Throughout my time as a CORE member, they have always believed in me more than I believe in myself.

So, I signed up for coaching and was accepted. I remember asking my first coach, "How do I save $100,000 a year?" He looked at me like I was crazy and said, "That's easy. You call your financial planner and tell him to auto draft $8,333 from your paycheck each month and invest it for you." The answers from CORE coaches are always simple. The work is not easy, but it's also not complicated.

When I first joined, I found myself overwhelmed at times with the forms and homework. My business was messy, and outside of what my loan origination software did for me, I hadn't been tracking any leads, production or expenses, and I didn't keep a budget. So, the organization was tough at times. I was used to being a wildcard! The good news was, I didn't find it difficult to surrender because my coaches were making more money than me, were working fewer hours than me, saved a lot more money than me, and had better businesses. I believed that if I did what they told me, I could have those things, too. So, I didn't fight them in their coaching.

I came to coaching with the belief that my team was broken. However, Rick told me, "There are no bad employees, only bad leaders." That comment changed my whole belief system, and at that moment, leadership became my number one responsibility. Everything from there is just simple details and processes.

In my first three years at The CORE, my average loan size doubled, my production tripled, and my income increased fivefold. My work environment is more organized, my team is the biggest and tightest it's ever been, and we're helping more families get into homes than I had ever thought possible. I've always loved what I do, and now I get to do more of the things I enjoy, and I'm having more fun now than I've ever had. I'm surrounded by the best of the best, both at my company and at The CORE.

Now, I'm focused, and I'm moving in a direction. I'm not successful by accident – My business is on purpose, and I'm no longer a wildcard. The most important lessons I've learned are: Do my best. Do the right thing. Show people I care. Leadership is my number one responsibility because it's all about influencing people and impacting lives. As I design the details of my future, The CORE keeps my perspective in check. The people I'm surrounded by will not let me fail, so I'm doing things I never thought possible because I'm not afraid of failing.

I'm a blessed woman.

# Dixie Sanders

## Lender Coach

**Location**: Sugarland, Texas

**Started with The CORE**: January 2004

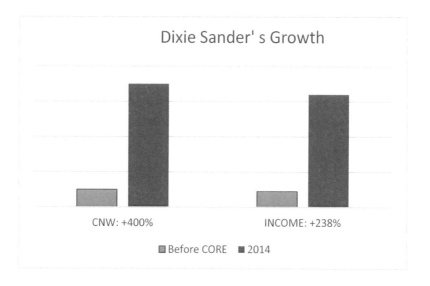

# Dixie Sanders

In September 2004, I received a call from a friend of mine, a mortgage banker, who asked if I wanted to attend The CORE Event in San Antonio. Prior to that call, I had never heard of The CORE or Rick Ruby. She explained to me that it was some crazy, high-cost coaching program, and that we would just go to the event, but we would not join coaching. Since we had become seminar junkies, and it was not far away and was at a really nice hotel, I said "Why not!"

So off we went to San Antonio, Texas. I had never in my career been to any event or seminar that was so impressive. Rick Ruby and the other coaches were dynamic, and I had never learned so much. By the end of the second day, we were hooked. Being the driven professional I am, I then had to figure out how I was going to sell this to my spouse. We work together, and we both had seen "coaching programs" or "life coaches" that were long on promises and short on delivery. Initially, he was skeptical. He would tease me, standing rigidly at attention in my office, his voice booming the last traces of General Douglas MacArthur's farewell speech to the Corps of Cadets at West Point, "… when I cross the river, my last conscious thoughts will be of the Corps, and the Corps, and the Corps."

A couple of days after I got home from the seminar, I told my husband that I was going to join this coaching program. He asked about the cost for coaching, and he teasingly offered to be my coach, saying, "Well, I can tell you what to do," knowing that would never happen!

But, then we began to drill down to details and ask questions. What was great about The CORE? How were they different or better than other coaching programs? We were both impressed with Rick Ruby's brutal honesty, his direct approach, and his transparency, all traits he demands not only from his coaches but also their students. It was evident that truthful accountability was the foundation of The CORE. As my husband is always supportive, he agreed that I should join The CORE. I began my relationship with The CORE, and it has been a journey, bringing me more personal and professional success than I could have ever imagined.

The CORE has taught me and helped me to create balance, earning more, and working more effectively. It has taught me to build a team, bringing less stress to my life. Before I joined The CORE, I was foolishly prideful, bragging that I worked at least six to seven days a week, usually 12-hour days. Prior to origination, my initial mortgage background was operations, so I tended to find comfort in hiding my face behind stacks of loan files. Rick taught me that being the "highest paid processor in the U.S." was not a good thing.

You see, I am a teacher's kid from a small town in Upstate New York. My Dad retired from 27 years of teaching at final salary of $37,000 and nominal savings. I now earn well above my dreams and consistently save 20 to 30% of our monthly income. I remember, long ago, I thought if I could just make $50,000 a year, I would be rich. We all place a ceiling above our heads, allowing our smallest dreams to become our largest barriers. The CORE has helped me recognize that it is ourselves that hold us back the most.

After 18 months of being coached at The CORE, I realized that The CORE needed a female mortgage coach. So, I approached Rick and said, "You need a woman on your team." He agreed, and the rest is history. I have been a coach since that following semester, and I don't think there is any greater honor. Coaching is a true pleasure and a way for me to give back, hoping to positively change the lives of others as I have been likewise blessed. I only hope that my students learn as much from me as I learn from them. The friendships that I have in The CORE are some of the most rewarding and they are priceless.

Coaching has changed my life and business. Let's be crystal clear. I did not surrender easily to change, and I still have my moments of flawed logic, where I think I know better or have a short cut. But, humans are the most adaptive of God's creations and learn we must. I now work less than 40 hours a week and close 300 loans a year. The CORE has taught me how to build a great team that is invaluable for measurable growth. I am very proud of them as they also set the standard for all others – the "can do" professionals. It is amazing the service we provide and how we positively change lives every day.

Rick Ruby, thank for your vision and allowing me to be a part of it. You and The CORE have changed my life beyond my wildest dreams. My life is abundant. As we all must one day answer the final roll call, my last fond thoughts will be of The CORE, The CORE, and The CORE.

# Dayton Schrader

## Realtor Coach

**Location**: San Antonio, Texas

**Started with The CORE**: January 2004

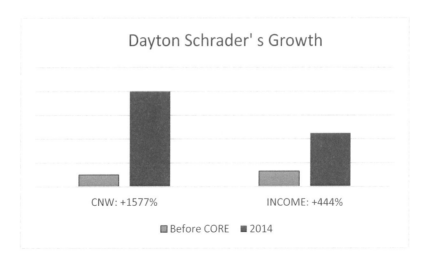

# Dayton Schrader

Da Na Na Na Na

If you are over forty, you will recognize the first few bars of George Thourgood's classic riff, "Bad To The Bone!"

That was the "bump" on the cassette that introduced me to Rick Ruby. It was 2000 and I was in my car listening to the latest offering by Joe Stump and By Referral Only. That month's featured tape was Rick Ruby Unplugged with "Bad To The Bone" as his intro music.

On that tape Rick told his story. He talked about money, relationships, referrals, family, divorce, disappointment and healing. It was an amazing level of candor and transparency. He was a real person telling the truth about life and business.

Wow! I listened to that tape dozens of times and I was hooked. I knew that I had to meet this guy, and I was convinced that he could help me get to the next level. I met Rick in person later that year as he was getting ready to start The CORE. I knew that was where I was supposed to be.

To give you some background, I started in the real estate business in 1982. I had flunked out of college and was trying to figure out what I was going to do. My high school golf coach suggested that I speak to his wife, Yvonne, who managed a small real estate office. Yvonne told me that I would love real estate, so I signed up with her. I went to my grandfather's house, pulled out a sport coat and figured out how to tie a tie, and started in January of 1982.

The first house I sold was on Super Bowl Sunday in 1982. No one else wanted to work that day, and I was the "low man." Back then interest rates were 16% and going up. The economy was in a shambles and I struggled. My friends were still in college or living at home. I did not know anything, and my customers were several years older than I was at the time. It was brutal.

Then it got worse. The tax reform act of 1986, the devaluation of the peso, and the oil crisis took a huge toll on the San Antonio economy. If I would have had any money or options, I would have moved. I did not have either, so I had to stick it out. Finally things started picking up in San Antonio. The economy improved, my skill set improved, and I had become a seminar junkie. I had seen Zig Ziglar, Tommy Hopkins, and any other trainer or motivational speaker I could find. I was determined to find a way to make a living in this business.

When I moved into a RE/MAX office in 1989 I was the only person with their own computer. I had an IBM XT and I was ready to roll. I finally broke $100,000 in GCI and thought I had it all figured out. Wrong! I was finally making money, and like most real estate agents, I had not saved for taxes. Owing the IRS money is no fun. I would not wish that on anyone. The certified letters, the penalties and interest were paralyzing. That was also very tough on my marriage. We survived but it was not easy, and it was all my fault.

In the early 1990s things started to pick up for me. I was slowly building my business. I was still living month to month, but I was selling more, and I was consistent. By 1995 I was grossing over $250,000. I was selling three or four homes a month and doing $8,000,000. Then I heard about Joe Stump and By Referral Only. I was past the scripts and dialogue part of my business. Joe taught systems. I was introduced to the concepts of "Before, During and After." Joe also taught about turbulence, the reticular activator, Fred the Head, and much more. I was stoked. I came home and threw away my pager, took my home number off my cards, quit doing open houses and stopped taking phone duty. I was going to be "By Referral Only."

I had purchased a lap top and Top Producer. I hired my first assistant and my business start to take off. I went from $8,000,000 to $15,000,000, and I was the number one agent in my office and one of the top 5 in San Antonio. It was a nice run and I was feeling pretty good about myself, until I heard that tape.

I was making money, but I was broke. I had no real savings and some credit card debt. I was okay on taxes (I had defiantly learned that lesson), but "okay" is not a very soft pillow.

Rick was talking or yelling at me. It hit me right between the eyes. I had systems but I had no structure or accountability. I needed a boss to tell me what to do and to keep me focused. I did not need scripts. I knew what to say and when to say it. I could process a transaction. I just did not have anything to show for it but a bunch of plaques. Big whoop!

Listening to Rick was a life changer for me. I learned to do a profit & loss and a personal budget each month. I learned to track every lead and my net and gross on every transaction. I learned how and when to hire staff. I learned to run a profitable business. I also learned how to sell. Really sell. I just thought that I knew what I was doing until I saw a real salesman.

I also listened to Rick on the personal side. I had a young daughter at the time, and listening to Rick speak very candidly about his relationships with his daughters was a great lesson. I was determined to learn from the lessons that he was generous enough to share. Life balance is huge with The CORE. We work hard so we can have a great life. We want to share, give back, take care of our families, churches and charities.

I got involved immediately with The CORE. I started doing the forms and going to the bi-annual Summit events. I signed up for coaching, and I did what I was told to do. I went to Rapport Leadership and became a Master Grad after I completed all three classes. When I met certain thresholds for income and savings, I graduated from coaching and immediately signed up to stay on as a paying student. The results were too good, and I considered it inexpensive insurance for a practice that was bringing in great revenue and profits.

The CORE started growing, and I expressed an interest in being a coach. I waited another eighteen months before we were big enough to need another real estate agent coach and for Rick to agree that I was ready. That was 2007, and I have had the honor of being a coach ever since.

I am still a full time real estate agent. I have to be or I cannot coach. One of the ways we are different is that we are actually in the business. I am not telling real estate agents about how great I was ten years ago. I am telling real estate agents what I am doing right now that works. I am also talking about my mistakes and what I continue to learn each and every day.

I am still coached by Rick and held to very high standard for taxable income and savings. Production is nice and plaques are pretty, but if you are not making real money, paying taxes on time and saving each month, it can be very ugly.

Since I met Rick in 2001 I have grown my business from $15,000,000 to $70,000,000. In 2014 I will gross over $2,000,000 in fees. I will sell over 300 sides for $70,000,000 in sales. I make a lot of money and I have saved a lot of money. I have a wonderful marriage. I have a daughter in college who I see often. I have a great life and great life balance. I am also becoming more generous. I have always been grounded and grateful. Rick has pushed me hard to be more generous with my time, talent, and treasure.

One of the best byproducts of my journey with The CORE is the friends that I have made. My students and especially my fellow coaches are some of the very best people I know. We share a lot, and it is a joy to have them in my life.

I could go on for hours about the impact The CORE has had on my life. Suffice to say it is one of the best things that has ever happened to me. I am still learning every day. I still make lots of mistakes, and I am corrected often. I want to continue to grow my business. I prospect constantly because I do not ever want to go backwards.

# Josh Sigman
## Lender Coach

**Location:** San Antonio, Texas

**Started with The CORE:** January 2006

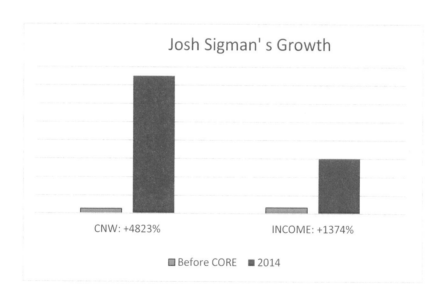

# Josh Sigman

To be honest, I have found myself to be quite average in most everything that I have done. I am tall, but I am not fast, and my hand eye coordination is lackluster at best. My friends describe the way I look when I run as a wounded giraffe. I did compete in sports, in fact I tried them all at some point, but considering the earlier description of my athletic abilities, I knew early on that I would never go professional.

I was a B student in school. I was probably a perfect mix of smart enough to do exactly what I needed to pass courses and keep my parents off of my back, and dumb enough not to push for a higher level of excellence. I went to college and graduated in four years, probably more because I thought that that was what you were supposed to do, not because I wanted to grow up to be anything in particular. I certainly never thought that I would hit the level of "success" that I have achieved with the help of The CORE.

My CORE story began with a series of accidents. After graduating from Trinity University in 2001 with a GPA in the low 3's, I had $50,000 in student loan debt, $17,000 in car debt, and I could not get a job. At that time, I thought that I would become a stock broker. It turned out that looking for a job in this field immediately following the tech stock crash was a demonstration in poor timing (it certainly couldn't have been my average

GPA). So, I got the only job I could get. Looking down the barrel of student loan repayments I joined the world of insurance as a commission-based salesman. I never pictured myself in commission sales, but it was the first of a series of blessings.

With the help of my first sales boss and mentor, and purely out of necessity, I became a student of sales. In my position selling life, health, and long-term care, I learned the art of phone sales: that if you call enough random people and ask them to do business, strangely enough, some of them will say yes. I learned for the first time that I had a skill set that was above average; I had little to no fear of cold calling, and found myself quickly rising to the top producer ranks at my company.

However, I was selling death and dying, and as a 23 year old, I was looking for more. It turned out that my college roommate and best friend had met (and eventually married) a lovely lady whose mother owned a mortgage company. So, while I was selling insurance, he was learning how to sling mortgages. One day as we were comparing sales stories and paychecks, Carson said, "If you can sell life and death insurances, you can sell mortgages. Why don't you join our company?" A short time later, I joined the rank and file of the mortgage Industry.

Most of us know that in this industry, a third is joining, a third is leaving, and a third is in it for life. My first two years were difficult, really just making mistake after mistake, which is typically how I learn. I ended up refinancing half of my block just by walking the dog with my wife and telling everyone what I was doing to stay afloat. Through the support of my friend, I survived the first few years.

What I didn't realize at the time was that I was missing a competitive sales culture, something that I had enjoyed while selling insurance. Again, through luck I was given an introduction to Dan Diepenhorst, the owner of Legacy Mutual Mortgage. Having already been in the industry for a decade, his business model was built around catering to builders. He needed help covering some of his builder relationships, and I was looking for a change.

I made the move and fell into a new level of leads, deals, and the problems that they bring. One of the best things that ever happened to me was sitting in an adjacent office to Dan, a monster producer, and listening to what he said and how he said it. The commonality between insurance and lending finally became apparent. You do not have to be the snow plow, finding a new way to do things, because it is easier to simply follow the snow plow, doing and saying exactly what successful people are already doing and saying.

For the next two and a half years, a side-by-side competitive spirit was born. It amazes me that competitors chase those who outperform them. Each year that Dan was still in production, our volume was within a million of each another… year, after year, after year. That continued until a local real estate agent invited Dan out to some strange, new coaching retreat. Upon his return, there was a new fire in his eyes. He told me that he had just signed up for a $2,000 per month coaching program, and I told him, in less flattering words, that he was "out of his freaking mind." I made fun of him for a few months, but watched with curiosity as he slowly grew his personal production and ultimately beat me soundly that year. He was doing something different, and it was working!

In May of 2006, Dan made it a requirement that I attend the CORE Summit in Colorado. At the time, I was producing roughly $18 million in production, which made me a very well paid young professional for the sleepy town of San Antonio. As a 26-year-old man, I was already able to save and live in a comfortable manor, and to be honest, I thought it was possible that I had already achieved the top levels of what our industry had to offer.

I was wrong.

The Summit started with a crazy, short, wiry, wild-eyed man yelling at the group that we were "all doing it wrong…that we were all confused." The founder of The CORE and my mentor to this day, Rick Ruby, said that he could prove to us that he was right and we were wrong. We were asked to write down our income, cash net worth, and total net worth. We were then asked to pass our information to the person to the right. Each at the table was to read the results out loud to the group. Rick believes in the bigger pile theory. If someone in the industry does more, makes more, and saves more, in fewer hours, and with a servant's heart, you have something to learn from that person. I was astonished to find that at my table of eight, I was the lowest earner and saver. As it turned out, everyone else at my table was either a CORE coach or CORE student, and a full half of the people at my table were already millionaires. Dan still laughs at me to this day because my jaw did not come off the floor for ten minutes.

The result of that moment was twofold: First, the limit of what I thought was possible in the industry was forever shattered. Now, I believe that if you can dream it, you can achieve it. Second, my tablemates were so different from each other. They were skinny, fat, smart, not so smart, male, female, and from all over the country. The only common denominator was The CORE. What I thought in that moment was that if these people could do it, I could do it. I was hooked. After an amazing two days of learning tactics and techniques on how to run a better business, Dan and I retreated for a fireside drink and cigar. Dan's wife snapped a picture of us that captured the moment I looked at Dan and said that we would both be millionaires. With the help of the Summit, it was also the first time that I actually believed it was possible.

On the plane ride home, my head was spinning. I felt like I had been drinking water from a fire hose for the last 48 hours, and I did not know where to start. I knew that the blinders had been lifted off, but the task in front of me was daunting. At that time, I was working 70-80 hours a week, had less than 12 months' reserves in the bank, was a newlywed, and had zero assistants. The service I provided to my customers was average, and it had the feeling of being transactional. I had zero faith in a higher power, treated my body recklessly, and had no purpose. I was a ship adrift in the night and good fortune alone had kept me, thus far, out of harm's way.

My first homework assignment to myself was to hire an assistant. I knew that in order to decrease my hours and give better service to my clients, I had no choice. At the same time, I wrote a thank you letter to myself from a client five years in the future who had just finished a home loan with my team, describing in vivid detail how wonderful the loan process was. At that first Summit, The CORE taught me that it is easier to get to your goal if you know what that goal actually looks and feels like. I took the CORE Score Test home with me to study. This is a test given at the Summit that evaluates where you are in your sales, team building, and personal wealth. Out of a possible 60 points on that first test, I scored a three. I figured that if I just turned two "no's" to "yes's" every month, by the end of the year, my business would be significantly better. This was my snowplow, and all I had to do was follow it.

It worked. Over the next 18 months, I hired my first assistant and raised my score to 30 out of 60. My hours were down, my customer service was up, my wife was happier, and I was making and saving more money. But I still wasn't satisfied with my progress. Looking back, I realize that I was smart enough to follow the road map, I was just not accomplishing the tasks as fast as I was hoping.

The missing link was accountability. While I attended the Summits every six months, I had not gone "all in" and actually joined as a coaching member. The perceived high cost of coaching was something I could not understand. It was actually two and a half times my mortgage, and I thought I could do what was required without the cost. I was wrong again.

As it turns out, accountability is the most important piece to the puzzle. We all know the theory of what it takes to lose weight. All you have to do is eat less and work out more. Why is it then that the majority of Americans are obese? What I noticed is that the best actors, athletes, businesspeople, and leaders are all accountable to coaches. It IS the difference between good and GREAT!

I knew I had to up my level of commitment if I was ever going to achieve what I defined as true success. After an interesting conversation about what it meant to join The CORE, and a glass or two of liquid courage, I approached Rick Ruby and told him that I would not only be a fantastic student, but I would be a future coach if he accepted me into his program.

I felt very privileged to have been accepted into this elite group of individuals. I knew that I did not just want to be part of the fraternity, but wanted to make sure that as a business person, the dollars I spent paid dividends. In other words, what I did early in the process, and the most successful students have done as well, is to SURRENDER to The CORE's coaches and systems. I believed that they had a better system than I, and I was willing to stop doing business the way that I had been doing it. I was willing to get uncomfortable, because my belief was so strong in what The CORE philosophy and systems were that I had to admit to myself that I was broken. This was very difficult for me, but I believe that it was a huge milestone on the path to where my business is today.

The first step in coaching is determining your six-month goals for income, assets, volume, units, vacation time, giving to charity, and hours worked. I did so and then picked the top two things that I HAD to accomplish in the next 6 months and attached a consequence to not achieving those goals. I was committed, but looking back, I did not realize how committed I was to going to the next level.

Everyone who knows me knows that I love to hunt and fish. It is what I want to be doing if I am not at work or with my family. When I looked back at my first set of consequences while preparing for this story, I found that my first written consequence was that I would not allow myself to hunt at all, the entire following hunting season, if I did not achieve both goals. The theory is the higher the level of commitment, the more likely you are to succeed. There was NO WAY that I was not going to be hunting with my buddies that season.

Over the next six months, my sales-oriented, fly-by-the-seat-of-my-pants success based on sheer charisma and determination was transformed into a systematic tracker of all things relevant to my business. In walked the Blue Beast. The Blue Beast is the tracking system that all CORE students follow to better understand their leads, conversion ratios, average price point, average commission per transaction, P&L's, and personal family budget. It is called the BEAST because it represents our business: It will either eat us alive, or we will tame the beast. Tracking everything is the difference.

Every two weeks on my coaching call, I was hammered over the head any time I missed something relevant to my business or that might impact my ability to reach my six-month goals. Yes, sometimes it was painful and I occasionally asked why I was paying to be tortured. But, I knew then as I know now that the coach was telling me what I needed to hear, not what I wanted to hear, and that makes all of the difference.

As it turned out, I had a great hunting season.

My two years as a coaching student flew by. Keeping things simple, following the roadmap, and being held accountable resulted in a decrease in my hours from 75 hours a week to 50, a tripling of my savings, a loan volume increase of 50 percent, and an income increase from $140,000 to $450,000. My only regret was that I had not signed up for coaching sooner.

As I had hoped, I was asked to become a coach of The CORE training upon graduation. I was elated and terrified at the same time. As a student, I was being observed, measured, and tracked. As a coach, I was and still am under a microscope. Flipping from a paying member to being paid was a nice perk, but I opted to coach for three reasons:

First, I believe that steel sharpens steel. I believe that if I surround myself with and get in tighter relationships with the principles and coaches of The CORE, that I will be in a position to learn even more.

Second, by coaching, I would increase my commitment through accountability. I know that I cannot ask a student to do something that I am unwilling or unable to do myself, which keeps me on track personally.

Finally, I feel a very strong desire and responsibility to pay it forward. I know that without my own coaches, I would not have had the success that I had in a short period of time, and as such I am responsible for passing on the information in good faith to others that can benefit from the unbelievable resource that is The CORE.

I have been in relationship directly and indirectly with The CORE for eight years now. To walk through everything that I learned or attribute to The CORE training, relationships with the students, other coaches, and principles would require me to write a full book of my own. Instead, let me list just a few of my proudest moments in the last eight years that I owe in part, or in full to my CORE family.

1) I found a relationship with God.
2) I hit a ten-year anniversary with my wife.
3) I have maxed out my college savings needed for all three children.
4) I became the number one lender in San Antonio for the last five years running, as listed in the Business Journal.
5) My personal production has reached $90 million.
6) I was offered ownership in Legacy Mutual Mortgage and now own 20 percent of a great company.
7) I have sustained less than 45 hours a week for three years now.
8) My team size grew from 1 to 12, allowing us to give an exceptional customer experience while maintaining high volume.
9) I made my first million dollars in a year.

10) I completed my first triathlon.
11) I became a cash millionaire.
12) I got to take off a day of work to be a Watchdog at my daughter's school.
13) Many of my students made and became cash millionaires.
14) I take four weeks of vacation a year.
15) I became the number one student in The CORE.
16) I am became the number two student in The CORE, second to one of my own students.
17) In an industry with an average loan closed per loan officer of two per month, our company is averaging nine each month per loan officer.
18) I hit my five-year vision in three years and my ten-year vision in five.
19) I stopped working weekends.
20) I became one of three senior coaches within The CORE.
21) I don't answer my cell phone when I am at home enjoying time with my children.
22) To date, I have accomplished 22 out of 65 bucket list items.
23) I was able to help fund raise $205,000 in 10 weeks for LLS.
24) WOW

In typing this list, I was overwhelmed with three emotions:

First, I have a tremendous amount of gratitude to Dan for introducing me to The CORE and taking a chance on a young man as a business partner, and for Rick, the CORE principles, fellow coaches, and students for the years of friendship, fellowship, and butt chewing. There is not a chance on God's green earth that I would have even believed that I could have accomplished a fraction of this list in a lifetime without my relationship to the CORE family.

Secondly I feel peace. I have the financial peace of knowing that my family will be okay. I have the spiritual peace of knowing where I am going when I die. And, I have decreased stress by knowing that I am not alone and can ask for guidance regarding any issues on the home front or workplace.

Finally, I feel excited. I say this because I feel like personally and professionally I am still broken. I am still an eager student. I still look at all of the work I have to do to improve my faith, family, team, systems, health, company, and skill sets. I feel like I have just scratched the surface, and if this list was accomplished already, what would come next?

I hope that you, the reader, will one day look me up and down and say, "If this goof ball can do it, I can do it!" Good luck!

# Brian Smith

## Lender

**Location:** Sandusky, Ohio

**Started with The CORE:** July 2011

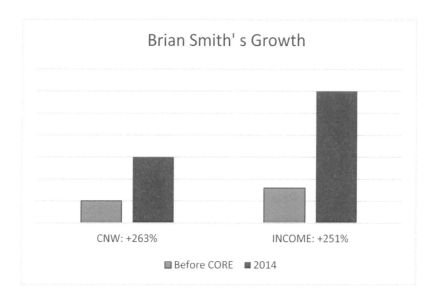

# Brian Smith

It was the summer of 1998 and a good friend called me up all excited one day.

"Hey man, I've got a job in the mortgage business up here in Independence, Ohio," he said. "I get to wear a suit to the office every day, and I get to bring in a brief case."

I said, "Wow, that's fantastic, man. Congratulations!"

At the time I was selling shoes at this sporting store and didn't really have much of a future, and I really didn't know what I wanted to do with my life.

So my friend said, "You know I think I can get you a job in this business too... but you've got to get a suit."

I think I had about 500 bucks in my bank account at the time, so I went down to Diamond's Men's Store in the mall and met a guy that fitted me up in the finest suit. I'll never forget that suit! It was olive green, custom fit, nice tight shirt, with a tie that I thought was amazing but my wife thought was absolutely hideous.

But I got this interview, and I sat down in front of this guy and said, "I'm an extremely hard worker. I can sell anything, and if you give me a chance, I'll be the best employee you've ever had."

He said, "I'd love to give you a shot. When can you start?"

So I gave my two-week notice to the sporting store and headed up to work on my first day. They told me to come in at noon. As I'm heading up, my friend calls me up and says, "Hey, don't bother coming into work today."

"What do you mean?" I said.

I had already put in my two-week notice, and I was ready to rock and roll. He told me that the company had just filed for bankruptcy.

"Everybody's grabbing files and computers and running out the door. The company is shutting down. Something happened with the feds, and everybody is scared to death right now, so it's probably best that you don't show up here."

So I hurried up and called the manager at the sporting store and said, "Hey, I need my job back. This mortgage thing really isn't going to work out and I need to be the manager again."

He said, "I don't know if you really should be here. I think you should continue to pursue what you're pursuing."

But, I convinced him, and I went back. For a good month or so I was selling shoes. But I'd had a taste of something new, so after a month I went and got a job at a broker store. I worked there for a good year and a half. Then I took my business to Wells Fargo, and I worked there a little while. I went through Sales Mastery with Todd Duncan, and got connected with John Maxwell and learned some leadership training. I went through some other different coaching programs.

It was November 2010, and a lot of things were changing in our industry. A lot of us were scared that we wouldn't be able to make a profit, and that our lives as we knew it as loan officers were all coming to a close. A lot of us were thinking about opening pizza shops or going down to the Caribbean to sell surf boards and drinks, all this goofy stuff.

Then I got on this end-of-the-year business planning loan toolbox webinar. All these different presenters had their PowerPoint presentations, their webcams, and their chat boxes. Everybody was sharing a bunch of thoughts and ideas. Then all of a sudden, this guy's big head jumps up on the screen. There was no PowerPoint, no webcam, just a picture of him.

He said, "I've been listening to a lot of these presenters presenting before me, and I usually don't do this kind of stuff, but I'm a good friend of Sue Woodard, so I'm here talking to you today. If all these presenters that you're listening to can't show you how to make $1 million using their systems and techniques, I don't know why anybody is even listening to them."

Immediately, I stopped putting my loan file together, I stopped doing my email, and I started to really pay attention to this guy. He said, "My systems are the best and my coaches are incredible. We believe in doing business by the basics of building relationships. We believe in systems, and structure, and accountability."

He said, "If you want to build a big business, if you want to make $1 million dollars a year or more, call me, call my group, and I'll tell you how to do it."

So I called Rick Ruby and had a conversation with him, and I went to my first Summit. Fast forward three and a half years: My income has more than tripled, my net worth has more than doubled, and my life is on a fast forward path to grow and develop myself and the people around me. Now I'm coaching six different groups of about 57 people total -- five real estate agent groups and one loan officer group -- on the 12 Steps to Your Doubling Income program.

So The CORE has been absolutely life changing for me, not only monetarily, but also in my leadership development, and in my knowledge of how to grow and build a business. More than that even, just being around some incredible people, the coaches and students of The CORE, has taken my life to another level.

Someone once asked me if I was doing anything epic with my life. I feel like everybody that is a part of The CORE is an epic person. They are world changers, people who want to do something and make a lasting difference, not only for them and their families, but also for the communities and the entire planet. And that's why I love The CORE. That's why I love Rick Ruby, Todd Scrima, and Reeta Casey – for changing my life and helping me change the lives of all the people around me.

Thanks. I love all of you!

# Jayson Stebbins

## Lender

**Location**: Morgan Hill, California

**Started with The CORE**: July 2014

Jayson Stebbin' s Growth

CNW: +210%          INCOME: +14%

■ Before CORE   ■ 2014

# Jayson Stebbins

## *"Starting to Begin"*

I am going to tell you a long story to lead you the fact that I am broken and need to surrender. But first, you need to have the history to know the severity… so here goes.

When I was 14, my father opened a restaurant in the town we lived in, and I have been earning a paycheck of some kind ever since. For more than five years I worked in my dad's restaurant with my other six siblings. I spent my high school years on stage as a "theater rat." When I graduated high school, my dad opened a second store, and I began to manage that store from opening at 10:30 a.m. to the evening shift change. There is no question that I learned how to work hard in that restaurant and watching my dad build his business. I was young, and I had money, but I never learned how to save or manage my funds. I continued to work, act, and play.

At 19, I decided to serve a full-time, two-year mission for my church. I served in southern Florida, mostly in Miami and its suburbs and communities. I learned and taught exclusively in Spanish, and found that my time in the theater and my natural talents made it easy for me to teach, communicate, and build relationships.

When I returned home, my father's business was in the midst of bankruptcy and foreclosure. I had a hard time reconciling the freedoms of self- employment with the risk, and I didn't know what I wanted to do.

A friend of mine told me about a company in San Jose, California, that was hiring. It turned out to be a mid-sized mortgage banking firm called Community Lending. It was privately held by a man named Darryl Fry who would become and remains my greatest professional mentor. I started working in the facilities department and was … wait for it … the mail boy.

At 21, I had no college experience, no real skills in corporate America, and had just met a girl I wanted to marry. Minimum wage was not going to cut it! I proposed to Lisa after six weeks of dating, we got engaged, and I began to ask questions of everyone at Community Lending to find out how I could get out of the mailroom and into a real career.

Community Lending had been developing a university of sorts to help train staff with a new approach to mortgage banking. The concept was unique, but required flexibility on the part of long-time mortgage staff, and it was meeting resistance. So the company began interviewing people to come in cold, start from scratch, learn the business, and show the old timers that if they could reach a rookie, they'd better embrace the change or they would be replaced. My questions were timely, and I was accepted into Community University as the first trainee.

From September 1993 to March 1994, I learned the business. I underwrote more than 300 case files, I learned how to document and funds loans, how to price, to ship, to insure, and how to sell. My experience in the restaurant, the theater, and on the streets of Miami as a missionary made me fearless when it came to talking to people. In April 1994 I moved my wife of three months to Austin, Texas, where we opened a prototype wholesale office in a market and a state where Community Lending had never been.

As fate would have it, we entered the market as the refinance boom ended, and every other California company was fleeing the state in cost cutting moves. Rates had moved up quickly, and by the time we got settled in Austin, I had heard from corporate that I could hire no staff, and I better make it work because there was no job for me anywhere else.

So I began my career in sales as an account rep who also underwrote, drew, and funded my loans in my tiny Austin office. The program worked well. I was paid on quality instead of volume, and because of my low overhead, I could work with just a few brokers, close 20 loans a month, have a strong P&L, and making decent money. This was my first real job as a mortgage professional. It was 100 percent wholesale with the occasional retail loan for friends.

In summer 1998, as my prototype grew to a thriving wholesale office and was being replicated all over the western states, I was offered a job back at corporate, back home, helping the CEO with national expansion. We accepted, moved back to California…and had our first baby. America!!

After that, my moves were rapid in the corporate space. Our offices ended up in Morgan Hill, the same town where I had worked in my Dad's restaurant, but we had no retail presence. From 1998, I moved from expansion coordinator to the expansion and recruiting team. I was recruiting brokers, and in 2002, Darryl and I put a five-year plan in motion for him to step down and me to take over as CEO.

In 2005, we formed an executive leadership team, and I ran all of production. In 2006, I was announced as CEO-elect and head of production, with a plan to take over at the end of 2007 with my co-executive vice president Janene running operations as president. We were doing $1 billion a quarter, we had 2,200 employees, we were in 44 states, we had $22 million in retained earnings and cash on the balance sheet, and life was good.

We were out of business by September 2007.

It was rocket stardom. I was a boy wonder, a mail clerk-to-CEO success story. The path I had set for the next 20 years ended with unemployment in November 2007. And the nature of my "broken-ness" started to emerge.

We decided we wanted to open an office in our hometown, Janene and I. We decided we would do it with Darryl as a silent partner, and a few others who wanted to stay with us. We had a bad business model with too many partners, but it brought us to Guild Mortgage in February 2008. We brought with us zero retail loan officers but ourselves. No pipeline. All we had was the database we had purchased from the failed company and a hope to build something great.

I worked very hard with the skills I had. The ability to build relationships allowed me to go from having no business, no real estate agents, and no clients to making the Guild Presidents Club in 2011. I closed $20.1 million, making it by just $100,000. The next year, low rates pushed me to $36.8 million and top three in California for Guild. Boy wonder was back.

But the reality is I had no process, no balance, no systems -- just my natural talents and some luck. That quickly became evident in 2013 when I closed $27 million, and in 2014 when I managed to salvage $27 million after starting the year doing 7 loans in three months.

Add to this that in 2012 we had a late life blessing of a baby girl. My wife cut back her work time, and then in

2014 after another baby girl, my wife stopped working altogether. I realized I had to fix our finances. I had to make more money. We were supporting our now larger family, her entire family, and it wasn't going to work on my income alone, especially since I was splitting all my income with my partners. (NOTE: This was a super broken business model built on overly generous and emotional decision making.) We were tens of thousands of dollars in debt with no relief in sight.

I heard about The CORE because the top loan officer at Guild, Shayla Gifford, was blowing up. She talked about it all the time. At a managers meeting she shared with us the accounts pyramid and other tools she was using. I spent the money to go to the one-day event in Dallas with some other Guild loan officers. I was enthralled, but had a hard time with someone telling me I sucked, I wasn't very good, and that I didn't know what I was doing. I was not ready to surrender yet.

I tried to implement some of the processes, tasks, and tools, but fell into the same old habits. I decided to go to the Summit in Scottsdale in November 2013, and I applied immediately for the program. I was sure I would get in. I was the ideal candidate. I had a phone interview with Todd, and he destroyed me, leaving me to realize I had no idea what I was doing. I was not accepted. I think it was one of the first times I had not won the day.

It was a tough few months after that. We were getting into more debt, business wasn't as busy as I needed it to be, and my partnership was draining my revenue. So I fought through, did my best, and went to the Summit in Fort Lauderdale -- the same area where I had served as a missionary and learned I was really good at building relationships. This time, I was much more humble, teachable, but still broken.

Rick interviewed me for my next application. He didn't want to take me. I pleaded my case hard, and he told me I had to get out of my partnership with my co-workers of 21 years. I was accepted, and I broke my partnership. It took a real toll during my first six months. But I felt like I could start. Now it was time.

I'm currently in my second semester. I know I have not totally surrendered, but, little by little, I am progressing. I will be light years ahead of where I am now. I am just starting to begin my career, after so much excitement and 21 years. I love my job, I love my journey, and now I am ready to take The CORE at its word, surrender more and more each day, and find long-term financial, professional, and personal happiness.

# Will Swallen

## Lender

**Location**: Houston, Texas

**Started with The CORE**: July 2011

# Will Swallen

## *"The Long Way Around..."*

In 1997 I graduated from Texas Tech with a degree in finance and economics, ready to take on the world. However, I really had no idea what to do with my career. Having very little guidance, I accepted one of the first offers I had, and began working eight hours a day – the American dream.

While I had graduated in four years, most of my friends took five, and a year into my career, they finally graduated. I began to see some of them land more lucrative jobs with greater freedom. I was quick to join one of my friends at a mortgage company, exchanging eight hours a day, five days a week, for 10-hour days and weekends.

Right out of the gate, I closed five loans, and I thought I was a big success. All five were refinances, since the company I had joined was a big proponent of leads. They trained me to "sell, sell, sell" with no real structure or direction. My manager advised me to work more with real estate agents and attend real estate agent events, but with no experience or sales training, I never really became a purchase-driven machine.

With years of what I considered big success, I changed little in my routine. Eventually I ran my own branch office of a large net branch company, and we thought we were setting the world on fire. I struggled with ups and downs and a few lazy loan officers. At the onset of the mortgage meltdown, I found myself producing fewer and fewer closings myself as I rushed around putting out fires all day long.

At this point, another friend of mine asked me to attend some round table meetings, and out of those meetings a group of us started our own brokerage company. I closed down my office and partnered up. We had a great 18 months of success, even in the height of the meltdown. After fears of losing our lines of credit, we accepted an offer to move our operation and become part of a local bank.

Shortly after joining the bank, I was introduced to The CORE, and I attended my first Summit. I knew before I went that I was ready to sign up. After years of the same results, I needed more guidance and accountability to help me implement the right strategies and finally hit the really big numbers. So, of course, I signed up. Luckily, I was accepted.

I quickly realized how much I wasn't doing, and I was extremely impressed with the sharing of ideas, strategies, and support. My first semester was a struggle, and my volume moved just slightly. But I understood that this was a building semester, and in the next semester, my volume finally launched. Fast forward three years, and I've made a change to another, larger branch with bigger plans that will now finally allow me to soar with the top producers. I have no more excuses and no reason why I can't hit every goal I set. I know it's all about prospecting, and even more than that, prospecting with direction and accountability.

It's been a great journey, and I'm looking forward to the next chapter.

# Ben Wilson

### Realtor


### Location: Mt. Juliet, Tennessee
### Started with The CORE: January 2011

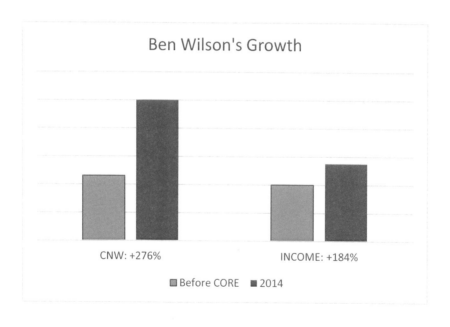

# Ben Wilson

Balance, structure, accountability, focal points...

I lacked all of these characteristics before The CORE. At first, my net worth was about 90 percent in real estate and 10 percent in cash/liquid assets. We only had one office staff and three agents, and I was working between 60 and 80 hours per week. After five years of growth, we had hit a wall and knew something had to change in order to go to the next level. Wow, did it ever!

It wasn't until after I started working with The CORE did I start to understand the changes I needed to make. In the last six years, man has the way I do business changed! The accountability and ideals The CORE brings is full circle, encompassing not just business, but all aspects of life – marriage, finances, health, spiritual – and it drives you to strive for the best in yourself and in others.

Being involved with The CORE has brought:

- **Balance**. Period. The main thing that was pushing everyone and everything away was my lack of balance. Now my schedule still fills up, but it is managed between the business and personal life. My date nights are scheduled; I don't miss my kids' games, practices or important events. My family is my priority, and everything they have is blocked off for them first.

- **Structure.** Over the years, I have gone from one office staff and three agents to five full-time office staff and eight agents! Having the flow chart and structure in place allows for us to work better and more effectively as a team.
- **Accountability.** The bi-monthly coaching calls, forms, and homework are essential. Without these calls, I couldn't have taken my business to the next level. It challenges me to think outside the box. It helps me see how others have done business and how it can influence how I work my business to the next step. The calls and the coaching aren't just twice a month, they consistently happen at the perfect time when they're needed. Being on the calls with other brokers and agents and knowing you are working with the best in the business helps you keep your game at the highest level, and keeps you always reaching to not just benefit your team, but the teams represented in the CORE.
- **Focal Points.**

All of those features: balance, structure, accountability, and focal points have allowed for a culture with our team that is UNBELIEVABLE. Truly, that is the only word that can describe it. It allows for an atmosphere that each member of the Team can *thrive* in, *grow* in, *learn* in. I have people from all across the business and in other arenas coming to me and asking to be a part of it. The team aspect is alluring and makes for a family atmosphere that most people never find on the job. We are "doing life together" as we call it. We are family. We are a life team. We don't just challenge each other in the work place, but in all other aspects of life as well. It's pretty awesome!

In the end, where would I be without having The CORE behind me? I like to look at where I AM because of them. I am now balanced financially, with 50 percent of my business from real estate and 50 percent liquid cash net worth.

I am more balanced.

I am more structured.

I am more accountable and reliable.

I am more focused on the end game.

I am always striving for the next level, and thanks to The CORE, so is my team.

# Amir Syed
## Lender

## Location: Chicago, Illinois
## Started with The CORE: July 2013

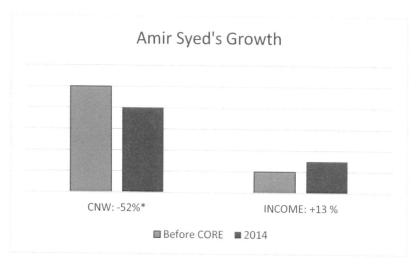

Amir Syed's Growth

CNW: -52%*     INCOME: +13 %

☐ Before CORE     ■ 2014

*Amir's numbers reflect a transition from an inflated focus on refinance business to a consistent focus on purchase business.*

# Amir Syed

I remember my final year at DePaul University, just a few credits shy of earning my bachelor's in Business Management. I was in a real estate finance class where a classmate and friend of mine, who was already in the mortgage industry as a wholesale account executive, encouraged me to enter the industry and even offered to open some job opportunities.

At that time, I couldn't wait to finish school and start hustling in the real world. During my study time in the downtown campus library, from the library windows high above, I would always observe the businessmen running around in suits and couldn't wait to get a piece of the action.

One Sunday morning during breakfast with my father, I asked him for his thoughts about leaving the family business and entering the mortgage business. I will never forget his feedback:

"Amir, you're young and living at home without any financial pressures, and your mom provides dinner for you every night. I left my entire family to immigrate here at the age of 30 with you and your mom and started as a shoe salesman making $3.75 an hour. This is a great country. Work hard, be patient, and build a great reputation for yourself. Everything will work out."

That was all I need to hear.

Once my father's support was given to me, I never felt more confident. I didn't wait a day longer to call my friend and ask him to make any and all introductions for a job in the mortgage industry. He introduced me to the owners of a small brokerage firm that had just launched and looking for young, aggressive and driven people.

My first step was to purchase a Calvin Klein suit that cost $300 and the "Mortgages for Dummies" book. My next step was to "wow" the owners at my first interview by bringing in Persian food for the entire office.

Yes, you read that correctly: I personally catered lunch to my first interview. The smell of all the kabobs serenaded the entire room. Needless to say I was hired on the spot and became a part-time telemarketer/dialer.

I was smiling 'n dialing, dialing for dollars, making the phone sing, whatever you want to call it. My responsibility was to call public records and convince people to refinance their high-rate mortgage into a lower rate with one of our senior loan officers. There was nothing colder than that type of cold calling, but it was 2003, and the housing market was hot!

I quickly fell in love with the competitive nature of the business and never looked back. My first actual full day in the business was June 16, 2003, the day after Father's Day and graduation from the college that I never completed. I had found the only education that had ever intrigued me, and that was earning a "doctorate degree" in mortgage sales. It was finally my time to suit up and get a piece of the action, and boy did I ever.

After two years or so, I had become the top individual producer out of more than 50 loan officers and also the top branch manager. My weekends were filled with dialing homeowners simultaneously on two phones and grabbing whichever caller picked up first. I knew that whoever picked up, no matter what they were doing at that very moment, would stop and tell me everything I needed to know in order to help them refinance. Our boss would sponsor $5,000 putting contests in the office for the top application taker and have a steak and champagne dinner for that month's top producers. It was such a fun and memorable part of my life. I was living out a motion picture, literally.

Fortunately, my parents, specifically my father, kept me grounded and had me save every penny. My father challenged me to save $250,000 in order to purchase my first apartment building. I set my eyes on that number like a hawk in the sky and drove towards it. It turned out to be one of the best accomplishments for me at that time. Otherwise, I would have blown all that money on homes, cars, jewelry, and everything between.

The next step was to save a bit more in order to have a strong financial backbone for the next milestone in my career: to open my own company. That decision came to fruition a month before my 25th birthday and right before the worst economic downturn since the Great Depression. There were many upon many sleepless nights. The mortgage brokerage community, according to the government, media, and mass public became public enemy #1 and the culprit of the global economic recession. Times were tough and there were many lean months.

Unfortunately, like many others, my first company dissolved just before its 5-year anniversary. I had veered away from personal production and was too far removed from the daily origination platform. Frankly, I felt lost and aimless. It was a very disheartening feeling to feel like a failure, especially for a competitor like me.

Fast forward a couple years and my entire group of about 20 were still with me, and I had committed to recalibrating and doing what I did best: producing and managing.

My first stop was Las Vegas to the Mastermind event in 2012. That day I watched and listened to Todd Scrima and Josh Sigman from The CORE Training on stage talking about earning more than $1 million in W2 income. It was like the "mortgage holy ghost" took me over, and I was hearing the Gospels for the first time! The speakers were very specific in their content, which I liked. So, I immediately did all my research, signed up for their Level 1 program and listened to every single podcast over and over again. I dissected everything, looking for flaws, cracks and inconsistencies in their content, but to no avail.

Todd, Josh, and of course Rick Ruby became like celebrities to me. I pictured myself being on stage with them one day and strategizing with them. I imagined being one of The CORE Training's top performers and coaches one day. I just felt like it was the greatest discovery for my career and absolutely rejuvenated me. I felt like a born again Christian, only this time, I was a born again mortgage man. I had found the treasure map and all I had to do was follow the dash marks to the "X."

In my first year with The CORE Training, my personal production reached $30 million in funded volume after starting from absolutely nothing. It has truly been remarkable. I know without any doubt at all that The CORE will take my personal production over $250 million in yearly volume and $1 billion in branch/company volume. The CORE provides the roadmap, experience, and accountability along the journey.

Rick has hosted me in his home and answered all my calls (and yelled at me every time). Todd has returned every single one of my calls. Josh has always given me simple advice patiently. No egos, no derogating. Just tough and genuine love.

I was taught by a friend that we are the average of the all the people we hang out with. When playing sports with highly talented athletes, your performance improves. It's the same with business coaching. The CORE Training comprises active coaches that operate at a very high level both professionally and personally.

If we only have a certain amount of time allotted to us in our lifetime and have the opportunity to earn millions in our industry, why not achieve great feats? Why even waste time or settle for anything less in earnings? That is foolish. Make the investment, join The CORE and get a piece of the action.

# Lisa Wells

## Lender Coach

### Location: Plymouth, Minnesota
### Started with The CORE: January 2011

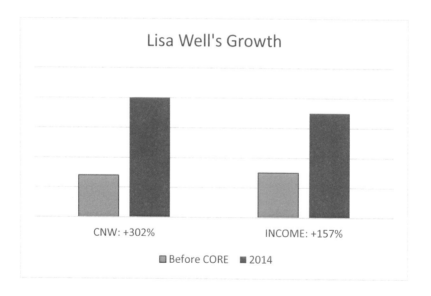

# Lisa Wells

"That sounds stupid... all that computer stuff. What I do is simple: Relationships."

Those are the words that I heard – and made me laugh – while listening to a Rick Ruby podcast back in 2007. At the time I was working at a large bank in their private mortgage division. I did a good amount of business. Suddenly, in 2007-2008 the market for jumbo mortgages took a slide, and my business was reduced to a third of what it had been. I knew that I needed to change something quickly, or like many of my colleagues, I would be looking for another sales job. Rick's words made so much sense. Secretly, I didn't understand the mortgage planning or computer-generated tax savings examples either, so I instantly related to him. At the end of the podcast, Rick offered a free 30-minute coaching session. That's when it all started for me...

My free 30-minute coach call went something like this: I didn't have a chance to say much more than yes or no. If I thought too long about an answer, Rick would say I must not have known the answer, and then he'd answer for me. At some point during those 30 minutes, Rick told me that my ego was getting in my way. He told me that just because I used to do a lot of business didn't mean I was going to continue doing a lot of business. Rick told me if I didn't learn how to do purchase business, I should look for another career. He recommended that I quit spending money because I probably made only half of what I used to but had neglected to trim down my budget. It was a rough 30 minutes.

I hung-up the phone thinking, "This Rick Ruby guy is a crazy, loud, opinionated, know-it-all." That was going to be the end of it. Clearly, this program was not for me. One thing stopped me from making the rash decision of forgetting about the call and moving on: Rick was right about everything. Well, almost everything… I only made a third of what I used to, not half. I had about $63,000 of credit card debt, two car payments, a house payment, and two kids under the age of two at home. Business was getting worse by the month. My career was at its tipping point. This crazy, loud guy couldn't be the answer, but I could not stop thinking about how accurate he was in his description. I agonized over his words for two months before I took the plunge and signed up for the Summit in Georgia.

"Where are you going and what is this for? You know what to do. You've been in the mortgage business for eight years! Just do it and quit complaining about it."

Those were my husband Kevin's words. Kevin is a disciplined person that never procrastinates – ever. He didn't understand my need for coaching or more training. I was already successful in his eyes. The truth was, deep down, I knew I didn't understand how to work in the new world of purchase. I was good at the mortgage business based solely on personality and luck. I had no tactics, no business plan, and no idea of how sales worked.

I was a college grad who planned to go to law school but never did (another example of me starting something and not finishing), so I began working as a waitress at a restaurant frequented by a lot of mortgage people. They thought I was great at sales and told me, "You should be in the mortgage business." My answer was that I wasn't good at math. Their answer: "It doesn't matter. Talking to people is what matters." Next thing I knew, I was hired by one of my customers as a loan originator. I did well in the business, especially during the refinance boom. Then, in 2008, refinances were gone. To survive I had to learn the purchase market. This was one of those "sink or swim" moments.

As you probably guessed, I signed up for the Summit because I chose to "swim." I knew nobody there, not one person. I saw Rick Ruby the first night. He once again drilled me with questions that I could not answer. "Jeez," I thought. "This guy is so in-your-face, and people hover around him like groupies." I was completely out of my comfort zone. I hoped the next day would be better.

On day two I met some of the most amazing people, most of whom were or had been in my exact situation – they were wondering how to survive in the changing landscape of the mortgage business, too.

I met with coaches who really, really connected with their clients. During our first lesson, "Everything is about relationships," I remember sitting with one coach in particular. Like Rick, he was bold, but in a much nicer way.

"If you join this program, Rick is never going to let you stay at the big bank," he told me.

I said, "Rick can't tell me what to do or who to work for."

"Have you met Rick Ruby? Yes, he can and yes, he will."

Then the coach explained how The CORE had evolved and how it had changed his business. I was hooked. I knew right then I had to be a part of this group. I signed up at the end of the Summit.

I was nervous to tell my husband what I had done. The coaching was outrageously expensive (more than our house payment) and we were not exactly flush with cash. Needless to say, he was less than thrilled, but he also saw how passionate I was for elevating my knowledge of the business and getting us out of debt.

I was not in The CORE yet. I still had an interview with Todd Scrima. Todd would decide if I was a good fit for the program. These people were interesting to me. They charged an arm and a leg for coaching, yet I still had to endure an interview to see if I was good enough to join. One would think they would be willing to take anyone who could afford to pay them. In the end, that was a big part of the draw. They don't take just anyone. I knew that if I could get into this group, I would be surrounded with people who were already good at the mortgage business and wanted to get better – seriously better.

Finally, I was "in." I was ready to start the transformation from refinance queen to mortgage guru. Well, the first six months sucked. It was all about tracking and filling out forms. They were hardly teaching me how to make big sales or learn anything that was a huge secret. I liken the first six months of The CORE to what I imagine boot camp to be like: They break you down so they can build you up, the right way. I was told that I should learn to love the grind. Who loves the grind? I was all about the bells and whistles. I wanted the get "business now" pill, but I was told to love the grind of sales calls and cold calls. The first six months were painful. Budgeting, profit and losses and pay logs… I was constantly being told I was wrong or I spent too much, or worse, my husband spent too much, or we didn't save enough and on and on and on… I learned the grind… the grind of being yelled at.

But, I kept coming back week after week for more. Remember the Summit coach who told me that if I joined The CORE, Rick would never let me stay working at the big bank? He was right. I changed companies during that first six months. It was a whirlwind, but these coaches were smarter than I was, so I decided to just listen and do what I was told.

Lesson 1: Relationships. Check.

Lesson 2: Learn to love the grind and surrender... Maybe.

My second semester coach was Jim Reed. His only assignment for me for the entire year was to cold call real estate agents. Now understand that at this point, I did not work with real estate agents, I was the refinance queen. And, if any of you recall, from 2008-2011 there were no refinances to speak of. This meant I needed to get the purchase thing going, and fast. I didn't know how to call on a real estate agent. I did know that I hated cold calling. But I still did it... week after week after week...

I didn't call on little agencies. I called on successful, intimidating, big agencies. There was one agent I will never forget: I had called him probably seven or eight times in addition to sending him letters. Finally, I got him on the phone.

He said, "Lisa, people call me constantly. They want to take me to lunch and try and earn my business. What makes you any different?"

I said, "I don't want to take you to lunch. I don't eat lunch with people I don't know. I want to meet you for 15 minutes to understand your business."

There was a moment of silence after which he agreed to 15 minutes at his office. That was five years ago. Today, he's my number one agent and a great friend. I was one of the first calls he made after he learned his wife was pregnant, and I received one of the first of their hospital baby photos. I have story after story like this. It was a grind to get to these real estate agents. I learned to love the grind because I love to develop relationships with like-minded people. That first year working with Jim, I went from working with one real estate agent to having 14 of them referring me for business. Fourteen real estate agents was a huge feat for me, but that still left my results average according to CORE levels.

My first year in coaching was hard. My husband hated the budget. There were many "money arguments." Money is a private thing to him, and he didn't appreciate people telling him how to spend ours. However, the coaching was working, and we were starting to make headway on our debt. In fact, we were actually able to save money for the first time in years. It took a full year and a half of coaching, the grind of calls, savings, budgeting, and tracking before my business started to flourish. After that, we began to see real progress, and my last semester, I started to coast.

The last semester of the two-year program was relatively easy. I was doing well, rates were decent, and I had found a rhythm. I started to build a team, which I had never really had before. I had people who worked for me, but I had never given them the ability to do anything except behind the scenes. It was always "The Lisa Show." With my last semester completed, I decided to take a six-month break from coaching. I graduated from the program feeling very accomplished. I had paid off all my credit card debt – almost $65,000 worth. I had saved about $160,000 and tripled my income. Not bad for two years' worth of work.

I decided to take a six-month hiatus from coaching because I had evolved so much in the previous two years. I just wanted to take my foot off the gas for a little bit. I had earned it right? WRONG – Lesson #3: I was a starter, not a finisher. I need accountability to finish. Taking that break during my coaching career is my one regret. I had worked so hard over the past two years. The great habits and sales mastery I had developed completely fell apart during my six-month break. I stopped doing a lot of the things that made me successful. I took several steps backwards. I think I was one of the first people to sign up for the next Summit and could not wait to get back in the program. I had gotten sloppy and disorganized. I attended the Summit again and immediately signed up for my next tour of duty.

I spent the next six months working on all the forms and tracking. Basically, I was doing all the things that had brought me previous success. I was happy to be home with "my people." I spent the next year working on team building and leadership. This was really when my bushiness started to explode. Building a team has been the most fun and rewarding part of my journey. I had an amazing team member already and remember hiring my second team member. I called Todd Scrima and complained for about 15 minutes about my next hire. He listened quietly and said, "You need to fire her. You hired a "C" player on an "A" player team… cut her loose."

This person had worked for me for only two weeks. The old me would have kept her. Her life would have been miserable. But, I learned to lead and that meant to act quickly. Within two days, I terminated her employment. I never saw so much relief wash over someone's face! Since then, I have hired four team members, and all of them are great assets. We have learned to sell the team concept versus it being "The Lisa Show." I truly believe it has improved our work and my life immeasurably. I used to think working 80 hours per week was great and vacations were for the weak! Now I think working more than 40 hours is bad time management and that not taking at least two to three vacations per year is robbing me and my family of a healthy life together.

In 2012, I was chosen to be a coach. This is an amazing honor and brought my business to a whole new level. I learned to teach by example and never give an assignment to a student that I had not already done myself. I learned to be a servant leader with my team. They questioned how much time I spent working on CORE coaching versus building the business. I told them that other people had taken the time to teach me, probably at the expense of doing a couple more loans, and I was grateful. Now it is my turn to give back. I never worry about sharing ideas because no matter what, I am always elevating my game. Teaching helps me do that. Being in The CORE has been an amazing journey. The CORE has completely transformed who I am, my business, my work family, and my home family. The other coaches have become near and dear to my heart and are now some of my closest friends. I can't imagine a life without them. We are all on this journey together, and we continue to challenge each other. I am truly honored to be part of the group as a student and a coach. I am fortunate to have met that crazy, loud, opinionated Rick Ruby when I did. His 30-minute coaching session was my tipping point. I hope the stories in this book will help you find yours.

# Mike Wood

## Realtor

Location: Reno, Nevada

Started with The CORE: July 2012

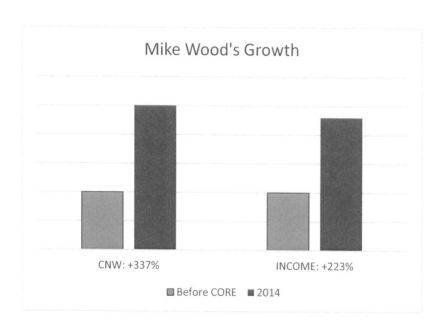

# Mike Wood

I remember it as if it were yesterday. I was invited to a CORE Summit by a lender in my market whose business seemed to be really taking off. I was flattered by the invitation and thought it might be a good opportunity to see what other real estate agents across the nation were doing to increase their business levels.

I was just starting to really build my own business, and part of me wanted to show off and act like a big shot, but I thought I might learn something along the way. I showed up early because there was a golf outing the day before the Summit and a dessert reception that evening I wanted to attend.

I went to the golf course early to hit some balls and found that my partner hadn't shown up. They threw me into a group that was short one player and I ended up golfing with a guy dressed in a lime green outfit. Everyone seemed to know him. I watched guys get something to eat, paying for each other's food and drinks while I counted how much money I had with me and contemplated whether I needed to spend $6 for a breakfast sandwich.

We started the round and the guy in green had a side bet with his cart partner, so I knew they were serious about the game. I had never been a really good golfer, so I was just hoping to have a decent round. By the 12th hole, my game had given up on me.

I was on my phone after a shot, checking email when I saw an email from an escrow officer about a file. I called her for some clarification on an issue and then made two more calls. The first call was to my client and the second to the lender. I was putting out fires, managing the chaos. But my mind wasn't on the game and it showed. I hit a chip from just off the green that landed in a sand trap. The next shot went into the sand trap on the opposite side of the green. Out of frustration, I picked up my ball and started walking to the cart. I wanted to get back on my phone to deal with the problem.

The guy in green said something like "You need to just calm down and focus. You have a good swing, but your head isn't in the game." I looked at him and said something to the effect of, "I'm just too busy to deal with a game."

And that was the problem in a nutshell. I had created a business that ran in chaos, which meant I lived in chaos and the business really ran me. I sold homes, I made decent money, and I was always busy. Always something left undone, something to do, things that needed me.

Over the next two days, I listened to speakers and attended classes. Everyone talked about creating and running a business that ran itself. I heard words like systems, structure, organization, and profit, and I realized that they had found a way to take what I was doing and remove the chaos.

The guy in the green outfit turned out to be Todd Scrima, one of the owners of The CORE. I heard his story of having two pagers and Post-it notes all over his office, and the most heartwarming story of all: his pager going off at his nephew's funeral. That's when it hit me that I needed what they had. Even if they didn't make me any more money than I was already making, I knew the life balance that they promised would be worth it.

I absorbed the model over those two days. I thought I could implement the systems to a large part on my own, and I could probably mimic their model without having to pay what they were charging to be a coaching student. My thinking was that if I could start the process, I would save myself six months' worth of payments and be better prepared to enter or start their program in the next semester.

I couldn't have been more wrong. I spent a great hour on the phone with Reeta Casey explaining my plan, where I was with my business and my life. She basically told me, you can try to do what you think you are going to do, or you can come with us and let us get you where you want to go.

I knew that she was right. I told her I knew I could dominate my market, that I believed in my ability, but I didn't know how to go about it, and ultimately, if I was being honest...I was afraid that I wouldn't know how to maintain it. After all, stars are their brightest right before they burn out. I wanted a business that was big in terms of units sold, total volume, and gross commissions. Ultimately, I wanted to be known in my community, I wanted people's eyes to widen when I met them and said, "Hi, My name is Mike Wood." I wanted my ego fed, knowing that the income side would follow with my numbers.

What I hadn't taken into account was the structure and financial side. In my first semester, my coach Dayton Schrader spent his time with me helping me with organizing my team and putting structures in place to make me more productive. We worked on job duties mainly along with focusing (me and my time) on my clients that brought the most to my business. During the next few semesters, my coaches each took me from where the last had along a journey. That journey included understanding what my business needed and how to remedy the shortfall.

I started my journey by myself, making just over $200,000 annually and working 60 hours a week. At my graduation, after just two short years, I had a team of three and had grossed over $650,000. I currently have a team of six and should gross over $1 million in fees in the next calendar year.

Those numbers were mind blowing before I joined The CORE. They aren't any longer, however. My mental shift, which is probably the biggest gain I have received from my association with The CORE, has allowed me to see that I have the potential to crush all of the goals that I had held as untouchable.

The biggest benefit from my association with The CORE, however, is peace of mind. When I joined The CORE, my net worth was around $300,000. I had some equity in my home, a rental property and about $50,000 in a retirement account. After 28 months in The CORE, I have over $150,000 in investment accounts, $200,000 in cash, and $175,000 in retirement accounts, not to mention paying down my principle mortgage and buying another investment property. My total net worth is over $1.2 million and my business is running by itself, which allows me to take time off with my family and turn my cell phone off when I play golf. I can do what I want, when I want, with no limitations. The ability to do that is directly related to my involvement in The CORE, and although it all ties back to dollars, the peace of mind is priceless.

I owe my life to those with The CORE that have gotten me where I am today and will take me to where I will be tomorrow. No limits and no fears, that's what they are about, and I love it!

# Lisa Whitman

## Lender

**Location:** Sterling Heights, Michigan

**Started with The CORE:** July 2011

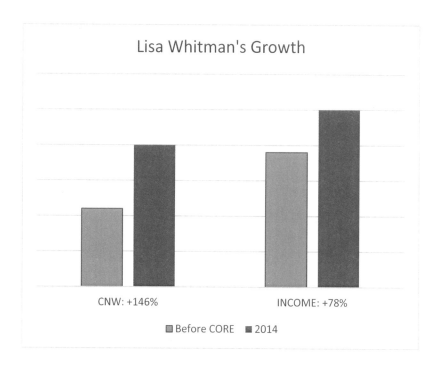

# Lisa Whitman

My life changed one day while I was watching a webinar on Loan Tool Box. The guest speaker was Rick Ruby. I had heard of him before because he always had someone calling me every month to recruit me. I blew off the call every single time, so I was intrigued to see what he was all about.

I watched the video and just laughed. He went on and on about how he hated the Internet and technology and that he couldn't believe he was talking to a computer. Then he went on to say what he thought were the simplest rules to be a successful mortgage originator. There was NOTHING I didn't already know. I was having my best year ever. He ended the call with an invitation to check out the Summit in North Carolina. I figured if he was that full of himself then this "Summit thing" had to be good. With one of his dialers calling me relentlessly, before I knew it, I had spent the money and showed up with an open mind.

The Summit blew me away, and I was practically begging to become a member. I was so nervous on my interview call with Rick. I am 20 minutes from Rick's Michigan branch, so I was a little nervous that he wouldn't want me in his backyard. He put me through the ringer, but eventually I was accepted.

My first 12 months as a student in 2011 were some of the toughest of my career. I cried, I had meltdowns regularly, and I had no idea how these coaches expected me to fit all this extra "homework" into my busy life. I dreaded the coaching calls most of the time, and I learned to wear pant suits when Jimmy Reed was my coach because he had me doing "burpies" in a dress!

However, my second year was awesome. I got into a great groove, and I finally surrendered and realized that these coaches were RIGHT, and I was WRONG and broken! When I finally did that, and opened up my soul to the process, it went much smoother!

My ah-ha moments and lessons I learned from each coach were very unique:

Dixie Sanders was patient as ever and helped me nail my budget. I love her for taking the extra time with me when I needed it. I was never so excited as when I finally got the columns to add up!

Jimmy Reed changed my business by making me do Tuesday update calls. That has absolutely been the best thing I've ever done to get more agents. He scared the life out of me, and I always felt like I let him down if I didn't get my homework done.

Todd Scrima worked with me relentlessly on my structure and systems and made me think like an owner, not just a loan officer. I was honored to have him take such a special interest in me and my shortcomings.

Dave Kammerer taught me compassion and how to love on my people. I would email him when I held an extra event or when an employee sent me a special message. I know it made him feel good too!

Scott Forman treated me just like a guy, and I loved him for that. He kept up with my energy and had me stoked on every call, and yes, I hired a dialer while he was coaching me. Game changer!

Shayla Gifford is my hero. I just wanted to jump through the phone on her calls. I think my model is just like hers or very similar, so I related to her very well. I implemented the video emails with her help and she pushed me really hard. The videos are a hit, and I will be forever grateful.

Jane Floyd was my coach when the coaching calls moved to video. It was awesome watching her energy. It was awesome to see that your coach cared. Jane called me when I was having a big builder meeting and was always there to pump me up.

Rick Ruby took a special interest in me early on and helped me with my P&L. I made a few trips to his Michigan branch to get my butt kicked about how I was doing my P&L wrong! Trust me, it only took a few times to mess that up before I got it figured out. My first impression of Rick was skewed because he rubbed me the wrong way. After knowing him for more than four years, I love and respect him so much. I am so grateful he came into my life. I have saved more money and have become more successful because of him and The CORE. From the bottom of my heart, I have never been happier to come to work because I love my job even more now.

A quick note about the special secret that these coaches have: It's all about accountability. I hired two other coaching companies in the past, but I never got anything out of them. They were jokes compared to The CORE. They would let me get away with not taking calls or showing up with assignments. I now cannot wait until Thursdays to get on the phone and LEARN, LEARN, LEARN!!

Lastly, building a team was very hard to do. After years of hires and fires, I finally have a rock star staff. That was never so evident until just last month. My father suffered a massive stroke in December 2014, and I left that day to head up north where they live with just the clothes on my back. I have been gone more than three weeks at the time of this writing, and my business has not missed a BEAT. I have had no messages that they couldn't handle. We closed 18 loans in December, and I wasn't there most of the month. They have stepped it up and I couldn't be more proud. I will continue to be out of the office while we wait to see what happens with my father, but the team has my back, and I don't worry one bit about anything when I'm not in the office. I have to thank The CORE for helping me build such a strong foundation.

THANK YOU for changing my business, my home life, and my future. ☺

We at The CORE Training, Inc. are committed to
helping you achieve professional greatness. Over the
past 14 years, we have developed a 92% success rate
with our real estate and mortgage coaching programs. If
you are ready to begin your own CORE journey, give us
a call at 1-800-660-6670.